GEORGE,
MEMOIRS OF A
GENTLEMAN'S GENTLEMAN

George Slingsby was born in 1889 in a tiny 'grace and favour' cottage on the estate of Babworth, on the edge of the Dukeries. Slingsby Senior earned ten shillings a week as gardener to the squire of Babworth Hall, and at the age of fourteen George entered into service, ambitious to outshine his father as a member of the 'inside' staff.

With fascinating details of a forgotten world, this charming memoir, written by George's daughter largely from the stories she was told as a child, follows his career from humble backstairs boy to footman at Welbeck, and finally as butler in the household of Osberton Hall. George's escapades make delightful reading, from the wager he accepted to dance the Duchess off her feet at the New Year Masked Ball to encounters with the King, soireés on the French Riviera in its heyday and his remarkable ordeal in surviving the sinking of the ill-fated *Lusitania*.

'A touching and hilarious book' *Daily Express*

'There are vivid descriptions of everything about manor house life — from constructing special lily ponds for the King's stay to the art of powdering one's wig before dinner' *Daily Mail*

'This is the real upstairs, downstairs' *Clive James*

Nina Slingsby Smith, the eldest of George's daughters, began to write about her father during the last years of his life. This is her first book, and she now lives on the edge of the Dukeries, only a few miles from Rufford Abbey and Welbeck Abbey, where her father began his years in service.

My Blue Notebooks by Liane de Pougy

Four Studies in Loyalty by Christopher Sykes
Introduction by David Pryce-Jones

Old Men Forget: The Autobiography of Duff Cooper
Introduction by Philip Ziegler

The Owl's Watchsong by J. A. Cuddon

On Sledge and Horseback to Outcast Siberian Lepers by Kate Marsden
Introduction by Eric Newby

By the Ionian Sea by George Gissing

With an Eye to the Future by Osbert Lancaster
Introduction by Richard Boston

Earls of Creation by James Lees-Milne

The Rule of Taste by John Steegman

Ghastly Good Taste by John Betjeman

Nollekens and His Times by J. T. Smith

Adventures of a Wanderer by Sydney Walter Powell
Introduction by Geoffrey Powell

Isles of Illusion by Asterisk
Introduction by Gavin Young

The cover shows the painting 'Tea Time' by Charles Hunt

GEORGE,

Memoirs of a Gentleman's Gentleman

Nina Slingsby Smith

Century
London Melbourne Auckland Johannesburg

First published by Jonathan Cape

© Nina Slingsby Smith 1984

All rights reserved

This edition first published in 1986 by Century,
an imprint of Century Hutchinson Ltd,
Brookmount House, 62–65 Chandos Place, London, WC2N 4NW

Century Hutchinson Publishing Group (Australia) Pty Ltd
PO Box 496, 16–22 Church Street, Hawthorn, Melbourne, Victoria 3122

Century Hutchinson Group (NZ) Ltd
PO Box 40–086, 32–34 View Road, Glenfield, Auckland 10

Century Hutchinson Group (SA) Pty Ltd
PO Box 337, Berglvei 2012, South Africa

ISBN 0 7126 9529 X

Printed in Great Britain by
Richard Clay (The Chaucer Press) Ltd,
Bungay, Suffolk

Contents

❦ I ❧

The Country Boy

George Slingsby, whose story I am about to tell, was born in 1889 in a grace and favour cottage on the estate of Babworth, situated on the outskirts of the Dukeries. His father worked for ten shillings a week as gardener to Colonel Dennison, the Squire of Babworth Hall. The cottage was very small, just two rooms up and two rooms down, with a stone cellar in which food was stored on one side and oil for the lamps on the other. It stood on the opposite side of the pictur-esque lake from the big house, a large, square building set in beautiful parkland. The lake also provided the Slingsbys with domestic water, which was put through a filter that just about separated the duckweed from the tadpoles, but since the lake was fed by springs and pollu-tion here was unheard of, the family suffered no ill effects.

Mr and Mrs Slingsby were simple folk, kindly and hard-working; they had to be, for the Squire was a strict master. Great respect had to be shown to the Squire and his family at all times, and whenever anyone from the Hall was encountered, the women dropped a curtsy, while their menfolk stood cap in hand until the gentry were out of sight. Parents were held responsible for any misconduct on the part of their children, for if the Squire's anger was sufficiently roused, a family could be expelled from the estate, and in that event they were unlikely to find employment elsewhere. With no Government help for the destitute, the only door open to them in such circumstances was the workhouse, and so their children were belted for the slightest mischief to ensure they did as they were told.

George was the Slingsbys' second son, the first, John, being two years old when George was born. A third son, Arthur, was born two years after him and as soon as they were able, the boys were given a few of the family chores. The ashes from the Hall grates were tipped regularly in a pit not far from the cottage, and they soon learned to sieve the cinders and partly burnt pieces of coal to add to their own stock. Nothing could be wasted in these hard times. They also chopped wood, carried water up from the lake and called for the milk from the home farm on their way home from school.

School was not a happy experience for George, and this was mainly due to the Welshman who taught him the three Rs. The boys called him Taffy; he was a man of irate temperament and a drunkard. He firmly believed that a daily dose of the stick was a necessary part of growing up, and if George didn't get a good hiding at least once a day, then it was because he wasn't there. The boys sat on long forms without back rests, erect, with their arms folded behind their backs. It was thought that this position promoted the growth of a straight spine. George could state with certainty that it also promoted the most excruciating backache.

One of Taffy's punishments for an offender was to keep the boy, after school, standing in a corner with his arms held high above his head. If the boy dared to lower his arms to ease cramp, he would be walloped for doing so. After suffering this kind of torture on one occasion George waited until Taffy's back was turned and then bolted through one of the high windows. The drop down into the playground was enough to break his neck, but the risk was worth it in the face of that agony. The next morning George's father went to the school and gave Taffy the ticking off of his life, while George stayed home and had his sore spots rubbed with liniment. After this, for a time at least, Taffy let George off lightly, and instead of handing out six of the best, he only got two.

Taffy, however, was not the only reason George was unappreciative of school. In his opinion there were always so many better things to do, and after he had learned to read and write, he considered the rest a sheer waste of time. He much preferred to search for the first violets, or to track a fox through the woods. The wood was his playground, and he knew every inch of it. He always knew the trees that would bear the largest chestnuts around the estate, and as his brother John felt much the same way about school, they began to play truant whenever possible. Other boys soon followed their example, and on fine mornings they would set out with their dinner bags on their backs, and meet up in the middle of a nearby corn field. There they would play to their hearts' content, until the train known as the 'four o'clock letter-catcher' came by, and then they would return home as usual.

Attending morning service as well as evensong on Sunday was something no one on the estate would dream of dodging, unless illness or some other good reason prevented it. The children also attended Sunday school, and there it was discovered George had a very promising soprano voice. He was immediately enrolled into the choir, and he loved the feeling of importance it gave him to stand up and sing. He received twopence every time the choir was called to sing at a wedding, and as he practised more and more, he found himself growing in popularity. People began to come from other villages to hear him sing and he wouldn't have been quite natural if he hadn't enjoyed the fuss.

Then Babworth estate changed hands. The new Squire, Colonel Sir Albert Whitaker, took a more active and caring interest in his employees than his predecessor had done and entertained a great deal, especially in the shooting season. In the winter months, when Babworth Lake was frozen over, there would be skating parties too. The gardeners, George's father among them, would decorate the trees round the lake with little coloured lanterns, and the servants from the Hall would serve hot refreshments to the guests in a large marquee. This was an occasion when the children of the estate could pick up a few shillings in the way of tips by helping the ladies to fit their skates.

The Colonel also improved the standard of living of those working on the estate. He raised their very low wages a little and allowed each family a quart of free milk from the home farm each day. He patched their leaky roofs, and generally made such structural repairs as he considered necessary. He even allotted a plot of ground near the old church to serve as a cemetery, not only for himself and his family, but for his loyal retainers as well. Previously a death in the family of one of these lesser citizens had meant that the loved one was put into the communal paupers' grave.

On pleasant Sunday afternoons the Colonel took to strolling round the estate, which allowed him, besides the exercise, to meet his employees off duty and to get to know them better. He would offer praise for a well-kept cottage garden and encourage people to talk about their families and in time those in trouble would come to him for advice. Unlike his predecessor, he earned everyone's respect instead of demanding it.

With his keen interest in local affairs, he soon became a magistrate. Here, too, the people of Retford were to recognise the work of a fair-minded man. Often the poachers brought up before him on the bench had been caught plundering his own estate, and yet rarely did he send a man to prison for this offence alone. He would wave a big stick at a first offender with a warning; if a man had merely been trying to provide his family with a meal, he took the trouble to find out more about his circumstances and even to help those unemployed to find some useful work.

It is not to be thought, however, that the Whitakers turned Babworth into some kind of philanthropic society. The employees were still expected to give a good day's work for their pay, and certain rules had to be strictly observed. Idlers were not welcome, and few dared to take advantage of the lenient justice that prevailed.

Sir Albert took an interest in anything military, and would open the park to the Boy Scouts for their jamboree. Often the Yeomanry would also make camp there. Several gamekeepers were employed, and the rearing of young pheasants went on throughout the year in readiness for the annual shoot. On these occasions, all the eligible men on the estate were given the chance to earn a little extra money by acting as beaters. The children who cared to give up their leisure time to search for pheasants' nests could also gain a shilling for each clutch reported. The keepers would then collect them and put them under broody hens in coops down the wood side until the young were ready to fly. With his knowledge of wildlife,

George could smell out a pheasant's nest a mile away.

All these little extras helped to swell the family income, for the Slingsbys were well acquainted with working-class hardships of the day, despite the improved conditions. During a plague of wasps late one summer, when the Colonel had offered a bounty of one shilling for every nest destroyed, George and his father would sit for hours in the evenings making their own squibs with which to combat the wasps. This entailed rolling up newspaper to form tubes, rather like fireworks; these would be packed tight with sulphur and other foul concoctions and stuffed into a newly-discovered wasps' nest, with a clod of earth on top, and left to smoulder and smoke out the occupants so that the nest could be dug up in safety the next day and the bounty collected.

Lady Whitaker became a pillar of the church and formed a group for the women on the estate who could spare the time, to help clean and decorate the church and hold little meetings between themselves to break the monotonous routine. She had, of course, heard George sing, and at once decided that he had great promise. With the help of the Reverend St Alban's daughter, who was a music teacher, she began to coach him. Several nights a week he would be put through his paces, and although he loved the extra attention from these important ladies, there were times when he suffered for his pride. Before a special service every effort was made to ensure his voice was as clear as a bell and if he should suddenly catch cold they would have him up at the Hall with a towel over his head, and his nose stuffed into a large jug of eucalyptus to breathe the vapours. There were times when he feared he might suffocate, and he hated the smell of it all his life.

The big thrill of George's childhood came when he was entered for the competition to choose the top choir boy of four counties. He had already collected a handful of certificates for various contests, and Lady Whitaker had decided that to win this particular prize would bring great prestige to Babworth church. Two pieces of music were required – a little ditty called 'Sweet March violets', and the other a religious piece of the contestant's own choice. It was decided that George excelled himself with the 23rd Psalm, and for the next few weeks he was drilled unmercifully.

When the great day arrived, George and his parents set out for Retford Town Hall where the contest was to be held. The Hall was packed for the occasion, and they took their places among the rows of boys with well-scrubbed faces. George began to quake, and Lady Whitaker herself was almost as nervous, but when his turn came he sang sweet and clear. Time and time again the contestants repeated their performances until the numbers were whittled down to the few finalists. One boy with a very fine voice had been tipped as favourite because of his previous successes, and it was clear that it would be touch and go whether he carried off the prize again. However, in the end, it was George who was the jubilant winner, and the many hours of exhausting practice had given him his moment of triumph.

❧ 2 ❧
A Family Tragedy

The tiny cottage, with only two small bedrooms, was becoming rather cramped for the Slingsby family now that there were five of them. The children were all boys, it was true; but the lads were growing fast, and that would mean, at the very least, a bigger bed for them. Yet there simply wasn't room for a bigger bed, for already there was only just enough space in which to get undressed. It was clear that something else had to be thought of, and soon.

At about that time the oldest employee on the estate died. He had been head gardener to Babworth Hall for many years, and had lived on the other side of the estate in a much larger cottage known as 'The Old Lodge'. Here seemed to be the chance the Slingsby family had been waiting for.

8

Mr Slingsby approached Sir Albert to ask if they could exchange their cottage for the larger one and, on hearing about their cramped conditions, Sir Albert at once agreed.

Mrs Slingsby was delighted with the prospect of their new home, for not only was it larger, providing another badly needed bedroom, but it had many other advantages too. For one thing, there was a slate and brick oven built in, which meant she could bake whenever she liked, instead of having to take her turn to use the communal oven on the other side of the estate; then the garden was larger, so that Mr Slingsby could now grow a few flowers as well as the necessary vegetables. There was also ample room for a few chickens, and work was started on building a hen-house. There were even two pigsties a short distance from the cottage, and they allowed themselves high hopes of one day being able to afford to keep a pig.

The boys thought all this a great adventure and were only too willing to give whatever help they could, especially if it meant a day off school. Their new home certainly did away with the chore of dragging buckets of water up from the lake. At the Old Lodge there was a well in the back yard, and for the slight effort of a few pumps on a handle, they could have to hand all the water they needed each day.

It was such fun piling their belongings on to a handcart and transporting them to the new place and they all worked with a will so as to get settled in as soon as possible.

Theirs was the oldest cottage on the estate, with a history dating back some three hundred years. In the past it had been a tollbar cottage and the yard, or 'pound', had been used for keeping stray cattle until their rightful owners came to claim them and to pay the fines to get them back. The gravel path to the main Babworth Hall

9

drive had once been part of the old road to York, along which the infamous highwayman Dick Turpin had made his flight to escape justice.

The building itself was octagonal in shape, with pointed arch windows. Mrs Slingsby hung lace curtains, and pegged a couple of rugs for the floor, made from strips of many different kinds of material from her scrap bag, and a large clean sack. These not only looked colourful but were also durable. She made patchwork quilts for the beds too, all stitched by hand, without the aid of a sewing machine, by the light of an oil lamp.

Altogether, the move brought a great improvement to the family's way of life. Living rent-free, with their free milk, and the new vegetable garden doing well, they were soon able, with careful spending, to put a few shillings by.

Two years after moving to the Old Lodge Mrs Slingsby produced another son, whom they called Alfred. He was a fine boy, but he almost cost his mother her life. In those days childbearing was looked upon as perfectly natural; even animals could reproduce themselves, and so complications were neither allowed for nor understood. Any difficulty was treated in a very primitive way, for it was almost unheard of for a woman to go into hospital merely to have a baby. If any help were needed in a working home, it was provided, for a small fee, by the local 'bunny catcher'. Such women were useful but quite unskilled for anything other than a straightforward delivery. They had no qualifications of any kind, and their only antidote for excessive pain during childbirth was half a tumbler of hot gin and a roller towel on the bedpost to help with contractions. They simply did what they could to help bring a new life into the world and in the event of death – not uncommon for either mother or child, sometimes both – then they would make the corpse look respectable to leave that world.

The birth of Alfred left his mother weak and ailing, and it was months before she showed any signs of improvement. Then, just as everyone was breathing a sigh of relief, real tragedy struck the Slingsby family.

It happened one day when the three boys were returning from Retford along the canal towpath as far as the lock. Many times they had watched the heavy lock gates working as they controlled the flow of water and the barges passing through. On this particular day the gates were closed. They had often seen the lock-keeper cross by the small catwalk on the gates to the other side of the canal. As no one seemed to be there to stop the boys doing likewise, they began to cross, with John as their leader. The narrow plank was worn in places and, halfway across, John slipped and fell into the deep, steep-sided part of the lock. At first the other boys were not unduly alarmed, for they knew John to be a good swimmer. They fully expected him to swim out, with nothing more than a soaking, and a walloping to look forward to when he got home. But John didn't come up to the surface. After a few minutes, the others grew alarmed. They ran to the lock-keeper's house and hammered on the door for help, but it took several minutes more before anything practical could be done to rescue their brother.

The keeper let the water out of the lock, while the boys stood anxiously on the bank. As the water rushed away, they saw their brother floating on his back with his eyes closed. The lock-keeper dragged him ashore with a boat hook, and then they could see why John had been unable to swim out. There was a large ugly swelling on the side of his head where it had struck against the lock wall as he fell. The lock-keeper did his best to revive him, while the other two ran to fetch a doctor who lived close by. But it was too late: John Slingsby, the eldest son of the family, was dead.

Someone sent for the police, while another tried to comfort the two remaining boys. With tears of despair and fear streaming down their faces, they watched as the policeman lifted John on to a kind of stretcher on wheels and covered him with tarpaulin. As if in a nightmare, they followed the policeman and the crude ambulance up the Babworth road and round by the drive to their cottage door. There was no easy way of breaking the news to the parents. The sight of their eldest son brought home covered with slime and weeds from the canal could have been enough to turn his mother's brain. It rendered her speechless for days, and they did indeed fear for her sanity.

The doctor came and, after a brief examination, wrote out a death certificate. Then the same old 'bunny catcher' who had brought John into the world came to make him presentable for the next. For six days he lay like a marble statue on his own little bed. There was no Chapel of Rest in George's day. Besides, it was thought to be indecent for a corpse to be removed from the house before the day of the funeral.

It was perhaps providential that Alfred was still so small. He needed all his mother's attention, and it helped to keep her from brooding over her tragic loss. Even so, it was a very long time before the strain and sadness left her face.

The time passed, and George, now the eldest, was nearing school-leaving age. His father began to think about finding some sort of employment for him. At this stage George himself hadn't the slightest idea what he wanted to do. Not that there were many prospects for a boy of his humble background. Most boys went down the mines, and those who acquired a trade or skill were the lucky ones. There was the possibility of going into service, but good jobs of this kind were few and far between. George's small amount of learning might stand him in good stead if such a chance came along, because it was always preferred that the boy should be able to write his own name. George's father decided to prepare him a little for this remote prospect by getting him a part-time job in Babworth Hall gardens. In this way his son would be able to learn something of his own skill, for Mr Slingsby was a good gardener who could grow anything from a cling peach to a cauliflower. George started work under him at weekends and holiday times, and he was found to be an apt pupil. He was keen to learn and not afraid of hard work. His love of nature now gave him satisfaction to see things grow.

At first he was given the most menial and tiring tasks, such as hoeing and weeding. He put endless amounts of soil through a sieve in readiness for the sowing of fine seed and washed hundreds of flower pots. He sorted boxes and fetched and carried for the older men. Many youngsters might have found the work slow and unexciting, but when George carried his first small wage packet home to his mother, her smile was ample reward for his sore hands and aching back.

The job continued over the next ten months, in which time he learned to do many more advanced things, such as disbudding and taking cuttings. But when he reached the age of fourteen and time to leave school altogether, there was no full-time vacancy for a garden boy at Babworth. George had to start looking for employment elsewhere. Each week his father searched through the papers for vacant situations, but there seemed to be nothing to suit him.

At last, after a brief and unhappy attempt to train as a signalman on the railway, fortune smiled on him. A garden boy was needed at Rufford Abbey, one of the largest of stately homes that formed the Dukeries, the home of Lord Savile. It was only thirteen miles from his home, and the advert had stated that no previous experience was necessary. George felt that the training he had received under his father might well tip the scales in his favour. There were many applicants, but George got the job, for a wage of £8 a year and all found. He returned home triumphant and for the rest of the month could talk of nothing else but this great and beautiful house set in rich parkland surrounded by forests.

Rufford Abbey dated back to 1148, when a certain Earl of Lincoln first founded it to provide accommodation for Cistercian monks. It was built to the glory of the Virgin Mary, and remained dedicated so until the Dissolution in the reign of Henry VIII. It had associations with such noble personages as the Earl of Shrewsbury and Bess of Hardwick, and monarchs down through the ages had been frequent visitors.

The gardens close to the house were laid out in beautiful patterns, like an intricate tapestry, each flower bed outlined in neatly trimmed box hedging. A magnificent row of lime trees formed a majestic avenue to the house. George, however, did not enter Rufford by way of the main drive but by a back entrance to the kitchen gardens, and there he presented himself for duty. There seemed to be any number of gardeners, men with different skills for all departments, including an army of those who did nothing else but sweep the drives over and over again, while others were kept constantly busy cleaning and servicing the garden tools. Fifty skilled and semi-skilled men tended the famous and aristocratic 'Black Hamburg' grapes which were housed in huge domed glasshouses. Peaches, nectarines and even strawberries that could be brought to the table at Christmas time were cosseted in these enormous greenhouses. Then there were the winter gardens, where other skilled gardeners produced exotic and out of season flowers in the heated conservatories. Lilies of the valley, huge chrysanthemums, orchids and many others were available at Rufford all the year round.

George was given a baize apron and instructed that his work was to be wherever a garden boy might be needed. In this way, he was told, he would receive a good grounding in all departments. He was a likeable youngster, for his parents had made a good job of his upbringing. His good manners soon made him a favourite with the older men and because he showed promise they took extra care to explain how things should be done. Being the youngest member of the staff, he also came in for a lot of good-natured leg-pulling too.

It took him some considerable time to find his way about this large estate and to find the shortest way to get from one job to another. He was made responsible for keeping the vast herbaceous borders free of weeds, and in doing so he began to learn the botanical names for many varieties of plants growing there. On one of his visits home his mother declared that he must have swallowed a dictionary.

3

In Service at Rufford Abbey

The Saviles entertained lavishly all the year round, but the event that always caused the most excitement for the staff, both inside and out, was a visit from King Edward VII. During the racing season he usually divided his time between Rufford Abbey and the neighbouring estate of Welbeck Abbey. Great preparations were made for his visit, and all the staff of Rufford would work themselves to a standstill to make sure that everything looked its best for his arrival. The red carpet would be rolled down the steps of the front entrance and the entire indoor staff would be lined up for his inspection. But once having made his grand entrance, it was well respected that His Majesty preferred to set aside a great deal of the protocol and relax like anyone else on holiday. He would wander where he pleased, and liked especially to stroll in the rose gardens, often stopping to speak to the men working there and to ask questions about his favourite roses. The staff who had been employed at Rufford for any length of time took it all in their stride and this included the sometimes disrespectful treatment of their roses by the King's little dog, which was never parted from its royal master.

For George, a mere garden boy, his first glimpse of the King was the biggest thrill of his young life. He had been weeding one of the long herbaceous borders when the King came strolling by. His Majesty didn't notice such a minor member of that enormous garden staff, but to George it was really something to write home about. He was a little disappointed, actually. He didn't quite know what he expected the King to be like, but he hadn't thought that he would look so like everyone else. He wasn't even wearing the State crown. On his next home leave his parents had to listen while he related the incident in detail, and they smiled indulgently as he predicted, 'I'm going to meet the King in person one day.'

At this time such a thing seemed as impossible as flying to the moon, but with George it grew into a burning ambition – to meet and, if possible, speak with King Edward.

During the first year at Rufford George made splendid progress, so much so that at the end of the year he was given a small promotion. He was put in charge of the herbaceous borders, to make close inspection of all the plants and to report any sign of disease. To George, this was a position of trust and he would have died sooner than fail in his duties. It also meant that another garden boy was needed to take his place and as his younger brother Arthur was about to leave school, George at once put in a good word to the head gardener about him. Arthur duly applied and was given the job. Both boys were delighted to be together again. They were even allowed to share the same room.

Arthur was put to work in the huge vineries, where his duty was to keep the vines constantly scraped against an attack from the red spider. It was a tiring job in the high temperature, and the bark-scraping was needed continuously. Later in the season, when the grapes were forming, there was the tedious thinning out of small grapes to allow for growth and this was Arthur's job too. The careful removal of ill-shaped and imperfect grapes was done with a long, pointed pair of scissors. The aim was to ensure a perfect bunch when the grapes eventually reached the table. Arthur spent many hours up the tall ladders among the vine nets, but he too began to take a real interest in his work and a great pride in the precious 'Black Hamburg' grapes.

By this time, George knew every inch of the grounds. On his days off he wandered around the park and surrounding countryside. He had never had so much as a peep inside the magnificent mansion. His chance came just before one of the King's visits.

Normally the outside staff stayed outside, but for these royal occasions the gardeners were the exception to that rule. The house had to be decorated and George was told that he would be required to help. His job would be to hand pieces of raffia and lengths of florist's wire to the older men, but he was thrilled that it gave him the chance to see inside Rufford Abbey. The more experienced gardeners were also artists in floral decoration, and on the evening before the King's arrival twenty of them, together with under-gardeners and enough flowers and foliage to supply Covent Garden market, went in by the front entrance. They all had doeskin moccasins on their feet to prevent damage to the highly polished floors, and wore large baize aprons with deep front pockets.

As they stepped inside the huge entrance hall, George was speechless with wonder. An enormous crystal chan-

delier hung from the ceiling, sending rainbow colours
dancing on the rich tapestries that adorned the walls.

'Coom on lad, look lively and shut yer mouth, you
'aven't seen anything yet,' one old gardener said, as he
grinned and nudged him.

They walked the whole length of what George thought
must be the largest and most sumptuous room that ever
could be. Without lingering, they passed on through
massive double doors, carved and embossed, to enter the
long gallery. This was some 114 feet in length, with a
beautiful vaulted ceiling. Two magnificent fireplaces,
one at either end of the room, were surmounted by large
Chippendale mirrors and the whole length of both walls
were lined with portraits of the many ancestors.

They continued up the grand staircase, and here, too,
the walls were hung with priceless paintings. One of
these masterpieces, the famous 'Boar hunt' by Snyders,
may have been worth a king's ransom, but to a boy with a
gentle heart, it was the most dreadful, cruel picture he had
ever seen. However, he was fascinated by the portraits of
elegant ladies in ruffles and frills and debonair gentlemen
in wigs and embroidered waistcoats. Their eyes seemed
to follow them as they went up the stairs, and again the
older men made jokes at George's obvious amazement.

'Thev got theer eye on you, lad.'

Another chuckled and added, 'Y'know what it is? I
reckon they're wondering 'ow the dickens he managed to
get past the front door.'

At the top of the first flight, heavily carved double
doors led into the grand ballroom – and it was breathtaking. Huge mirrors along the walls seemed to reflect an
indeterminable size to its already huge dimensions; the
floor was so highly polished that George could see his
own face staring up at him; and the reflection of four
giant chandeliers shimmered like stars on a pool. This
was where their work was to begin. Enormous sheets

were spread around the floor, and the flowers and ferns were all laid out on them. Then George watched enthralled as the older gardeners wove and plaited, entwining garlands along the balustrading that overlooked the grand staircase and decorating every possible space with gorgeous hothouse blooms. Silently he handed pieces of raffia, string and wire as it was asked for, but his eyes were alert to everything. Other gardeners were bringing in huge potted plants and palms, or were busy filling enormous porcelain vases that were set in various places around the room, until every niche held an arrangement of ferns and flowers.

They were to decorate the banqueting hall in the afternoon, so they were given a meal in the servants' hall, which was once the old crypt of the Abbey. The meal consisted of hot soup, large chunks of freshly baked bread and cheese, and a tankard of beer. This was the first time George had tasted alcohol, but he found it to his liking. He munched away, his eyes as busy as his jaws, for there was much to see. Servants from all parts of the Abbey came and went, all dressed in their different liveries and uniforms according to rank. Those who came near seemed friendly enough and, being of an inquiring mind, he took every opportunity to ask questions. The thing that astounded him most was the description of the unique pure gold dinner service of a hundred or more pieces, all embossed with the Savile crest and valued beyond price. He was told it would be brought out for the King's banquet and at first George thought they were pulling his leg. He found it incredible that anyone could actually eat from pure gold plates, but he was assured that this was so.

He took quite a fancy to a little parlour maid, all dimples and fun. She was a little older than he was and they talked a lot during the meal. He asked her about her duties, and decided that her smart black dress and white cap and apron must surely mean that her job was an important one, but the very idea brought peals of laughter from her.

'What me? Important? That's a laugh! Why, I'm almost the lowest of the low,' she replied, but added: 'There are the skivvies, of course, everyone is higher than them, but if I were of any importance, my lad, I shouldn't be allowed to talk to you.'

Then, to his delight, she offered to smuggle him in by a back door on the following night, so that he might see the banqueting table after it was laid. This was strictly against the rules, of course, and should they be caught it would be instant dismissal for both of them. George decided that if she were willing to risk it, then he would too. He began to think that his job as a gardener was slow and dull compared with all the excitement of work inside the Abbey.

The following day King Edward arrived. A stream of carriages, each with its own coachman and footmen in their different liveries, came in splendour up the regal drive. Perfectly matched horses, with their harness shining in the autumn sunshine, followed each other in a majestic line. As George watched the spectacle, he could hardly wait for the evening to come.

After work was finished, he washed and put on his only good suit. He presented himself at the back door where the little maid had told him to wait until she came out to him. He wondered if she would remember, but then he heard a movement and she appeared, holding a finger to her lips, and beckoned him inside. Just for a moment his courage nearly deserted him. What if someone of importance were to see him there? But she impishly assured him, 'Don't worry, no one is likely to notice you, and if they did they couldn't be absolutely sure you don't work here. Even I don't know everyone, there's such a bloomin' lot of us.'

Quickly they crept along a maze of passages until they came to an anteroom to the dining room. Peeping round the corner of those magnificent doors, they gazed on the splendour of the banqueting hall in readiness to receive His Majesty the King.

The walls of this great room were adorned with lovely coloured silk tapestries depicting country scenes, their colours blending with the Chinese carpet on the floor. Two magnificent fire-dogs occupied a massive fireplace at the far end of the room, where four-foot logs sent showers of bright sparks flying up the chimney. Four chandeliers, ablaze with light, cast a shimmering glow on the ornate ceilings and a soft brilliance over the whole room. In the centre stood the long, highly polished table, set around with gilded chairs upholstered with crimson velvet. Flawless Waterford cut crystal finger bowls, each with a rosebud clipped on to the side, and heavy silver cutlery winked and sparkled in the candlelight. George had never seen such an assortment of knives, forks and spoons. Brilliantly spotless damask table napkins, folded in the shape of water lilies, had been placed by each water glass. Heavy silver cruets stood at intervals down the table – and yes, there it was, that fabulous dinner service, each piece with its own glass lining to prevent the gold being scratched. The gardeners had ringed each plate with the heads of flowers. The crowning glory was the huge centrepiece, a four foot high arch over an enormous tiered dish of fruit and ferns. Nectarines, peaches, pine-apples and the most enormous pears, tangerines, green-gages and many other exotic fruits were intertwined with flowers and delicate maidenhair fern. From the centre of the arch hung an enormous bunch of the famous 'Black Hamburg' grapes, grown especially for an occasion such as this. The bunch would have comfortably filled a bucket, and each grape was the size of a small plum. A pair of gold scissors had been placed conveniently within reach of where King Edward would be seated. The little maid explained that the King always cut the first grape after dinner.

George felt a certain excitement well up within him as his eyes followed the slender silver ribbons leading out like the strings of a maypole from the top of the arch to each place at the dinner table. He decided there and then that, as soon as he could, he would leave the gardens to work inside the great house.

The parlour maid led him back along the passages and they reached the back door again without having encountered a soul. They whispered their good-nights and George made his way back to the room he shared with his brother, who was waiting anxiously for his return. Even after hearing George's enthusiastic description of all he had seen, Arthur still thought it was foolhardy to have taken such a risk. The only thing of real interest and importance to him was the huge bunch of 'Black Hamburg' grapes that had been given pride of place in that arched centrepiece.

After this, as he went about his work in the gardens, George thought more and more about how he could change his job. He mentioned to the head gardener that he had a fancy to work inside and the older man promised that if he heard of any position suitable he would let him know. But, several months later, it was his little parlour maid friend who told him that there would shortly be an opening for the position of hall boy.

At once he sought out the head gardener and asked his advice on how to apply for the job when the time came. He was told that he would have to apply through the butler. This George did, and for the next few weeks he was like a cat on hot bricks. Finally the summons came. The butler was a slightly portly gentleman, who received George as if he had a nasty smell under his nose. It was an expression that George came to know was generally adopted by all the best butlers. He asked him a few questions about the reason for wanting to change his position in the gardens to become a member of the inside staff. George hadn't realised before that he had the gift of the gab; on the contrary, he had always been rather quiet and a little on the shy side; but his answers must have satisfied this rather awesome retainer because at the end of the interview he was offered the job.

❦ 4 ❧
Black-lead and Boot Polish

A month later, George presented himself to the housekeeper, as he had been instructed, at 6 a.m. sharp. Now that he had burned his boats, he was tormented with fear that he might not succeed in his new job. When the housekeeper appeared his apprehension deepened. Tall, straight-backed and austere, she stood with her hands linked in front of her, while she ran a critical eye over him. Her hair was drawn back into a tight knot in the nape of her neck, and her dark grey dress with starched cuffs and collar gave her a forbidding appearance. A huge bunch of keys which hung from her belt jangled each time she moved. Then she smiled, which altered her expression so much that George felt reassured. She questioned him, as the butler had done, about his reasons for wanting to work inside and whether he had been unhappy in his previous duties. He answered that he thought he would have a better chance of making a good career on the inside staff and that his ambition was to get to the top as quickly as possible. She smiled again; obviously pleased with his enthusiasm.

'I see,' she said. 'But you realise there is a lot of hard work in front of you before you can do that?'

After George had assured her he did realise it, her stiff and starchy manner became more friendly. She explained that his work would start at six sharp each morning and that over-sleeping would not be tolerated. It would be his job to do anything that was required of him by any senior member of the staff. There would be no set working hours and when the family entertained he might be on call until midnight. She warned him that only his very best would do. Although his wage would be smaller than he had been getting in the gardens, his keep and clothing would be found. He would have a weekend off every month and one clear day off every two weeks. He would be free each evening after his duties were finished, so long as he was in by twelve. He would, of course, be allowed to attend morning service on Sunday if he wished.

She then conducted him to his room and left him to settle in. When the door had closed behind her, George began to explore his new quarters. There was a large iron-framed bedstead, covered with a spotless white quilt, two wooden chairs, a chest of drawers with a swing mirror, and a fairly large closet, where the housekeeper had said he would find his uniform. She had also informed him that the room had to be kept clean and that she would personally inspect it from time to time to make sure it was done.

Inside the closet he found two pairs of black twill trousers, two grey and plum coloured striped shirts, and a waistcoat in the same plum colour with smart black buttons. There was a large wrap-around apron with two deep pockets in front, and in a little trinket box on the chest of drawers he found several collar studs and a pair of expanding arm bands. Not really much as uniforms go, but when George had dressed himself in it he felt like a field marshal. Then he reported to the head hall boy, who in fact was not a boy at all, but a fully grown man. He gave George a list as long as his arm, but it was a relief to hear that these duties would not start until the following morning and that for the rest of the day he was to spend his time getting to know his way about the below stairs departments and familiarising himself with the routine expected of him – where cleaning materials could be found, and so forth.

In the weeks that followed, George discovered that the glamour he had imagined would go with this work was sadly lacking. It was his job to keep the huge copper coal scuttles cleaned and filled, and it took all the elbow grease he could muster to keep them bright enough to pass the critical eye of the housekeeper. He cleaned out grates and carried great quantities of four-foot logs. He took his turn to sand and scrub the long wooden tables in the old crypt and he cleaned most of the shoes in the Abbey. Then there was the mass of silver to be dealt with. Putting on the plate powder and then carefully brushing it off and polishing it could take many hours of work. There was no easy way to do anything in George's young day. What he hated most of all was the daily black-leading of a huge stove, and the housekeeper insisted that she should be able to see her reflection in the finished effort before she was really satisfied. It was a brute and the black-lead became grimed in his finger nails; no amount of scrubbing would remove it from the creases in the palms of his hands. It was not all drudgery, however, and he was not at all unhappy about his change of work. They were a happy lot on the servants' side of the baize door, and when things were not too hectic, they shared many a laugh.

During the next few months George made excellent progress and had found favour with the housekeeper. She seemed to like his natural good manners and the way in which he worked willingly and without complaint. The routine was fairly simple really, and he learned that nearly everyone had a certain status. Although the personal servants above stairs, such as the valet, lady's maid and the footmen, took their meals in the servants' hall, they were waited on by the other servants of lower rank. These lower servants were waited on by even lower servants. Skivvies at the bottom of the ladder, who had to get their own meals, were not allowed to have much contact with the rest of the staff and only left the scullery on very rare occasions. Cook was queen in her own domain and, although the chef was of paramount importance, he was not allowed to do as he liked in 'cook's kitchen'. The butler was in full charge of the pantry and all the staff connected with the domestic side of service, while the housekeeper had total control over expenditure and the general running of the house.

Whenever George encountered one of the footmen or any other of the personal servants in their smart liveries, his determination grew to rise in the world. He began to study the way they stood and spoke, making mental notes for the day when he could copy their straight-backed elegance. He found it difficult to contain himself every time these superior beings came within reach, but it was forbidden to speak, unless spoken to, which wasn't often. Servants of different grades were not allowed to mix freely. In the meantime, he was learning a lot about the workings of this great house and was gaining experience all the time.

One morning George received a message to report to the housekeeper, which usually meant trouble. He quaked inwardly, searching his mind for the crime he felt he must have committed. He knocked nervously on the housekeeper's door and waited for the familiar voice to bid him enter. To his surprise, instead of a reprimand, she informed him that the position of head hall boy would soon be vacant and hinted that, if he should apply, the job could easily be his. It appeared the present head hall boy was leaving to get married. In gentleman's service at this time, it was thought that staff who had outside commitments could not wholeheartedly devote themselves to the house they served. Most of the domestic staff lived in and wives were not catered for.

George was delighted at the prospect of promotion and gratified that the housekeeper should consider him competent to take this young man's place. He returned to his work with renewed vigour.

At the end of the month the head hall boy left the service of Lord Savile and two days later, after the usual interview with the butler, George stepped into the other man's shoes. He felt this to be the first rung on the ladder to success and he and his brother had a little celebration at the pub in Ollerton to mark the occasion.

Doncaster races were approaching again and this was to bring another visit from the King. Two weeks before his arrival, the great house was cleaned from top to bottom, both inside and out. A large and beautiful lily pond was constructed in the front entrance especially for the occasion. Fountains played into it and brightly coloured fish darted among the delicate lilies. The entire staff worked together to achieve perfection. George, this time on the inside of the lavish preparations, also threw himself into his work with all the enthusiasm in the world. The new hall boy who had taken his place was a nice lad, eager to please, and only too willing to do anything he was asked to do. George didn't overload him with all the jobs he himself disliked. They shared them as much as they were able and it was then George learned that it paid to lead rather than drive.

Piles of priceless crockery were brought out to be washed, and enormous canteens of cutlery to be cleaned. A dozen or more housemaids polished the grand ball-room floor until it resembled a sheet of glass and it took hours of hard labour with bees-wax and turpentine to achieve this shine. All the lovely antique furniture was given the same treatment, including that gorgeous dining table. A London firm came out especially to clean the chandeliers. Even the housekeeper, although still maintaining her rigid reserve, moved at a faster pace, and the butler showed his extra weight of responsibilities by an exceptionally high colour to his face. The chef threw a fresh tantrum every hour during the time he created special master-pieces of culinary art, and even the footmen seemed to have cultivated a special expression for the occasion. Their state liveries had been cleaned and it was plain to see that their day liveries had received extra attention too.

George was in his element. There was life and excitement in the air and it appealed to his sense of adventure. Again the fabulous dinner service was brought up from the vaults, and again George marvelled that it could possibly be pure gold.

The first evening of the King's visit was something that was to remain in George's memory for the rest of his life. The menu, of course, had been planned weeks previously, and so everything went like clockwork. As the sumptuous dishes left the kitchens, they were rushed from hand to hand until they reached the footmen, those splendid beings who looked like princes themselves in their state liveries, and they of course served them to the table. The food had to arrive piping hot, so speed was essential. To serve tepid food was an unforgivable sin. It was like a great chain going at top speed, with full dishes going out and empty ones coming back. Orders were being called from one to the other, and the head chef was as agitated as an expectant father. His chief anxiety was a specially concocted dessert, aptly called 'the King's surprise', and until His Majesty sent his compliments to the chef after the banquet was over he was like a cat on hot bricks. Later on, when the strains of dance music began, the staff were able to stand more at ease. During the grand ball their services were not required until supper was served, but no one retired early on a night like this.

Although George didn't get to bed before four the next morning, he was still up at the usual time with the rest of the below-stairs staff. Servants were not supposed to get tired in those days – well, not the best ones anyway. He struggled into his uniform and went along to the baize board where the day's duty roster was always posted. There were many jobs that never varied from day to day, but quite often there would be additional ones and all had to be completed before breakfast. Today he noticed that all shoes must be collected and cleaned; although this was an everyday task, it was the word 'all' that made the difference. George at once inquired if this order meant the King's shoes as well, and was told it most certainly did. All thoughts of how tired he felt suddenly vanished with the faint hope of his chance to catch a glimpse of the royal personage. The idea was dismissed almost as soon as he had thought of it because it was unlikely that the King would be up at such an early hour. Nevertheless, he still crept silently and hopefully through the house.

His daily shoe collection from the doors of the various suites had given him the chance to see something of the magnificent upstairs part of the house without breaking rules, though on occasion he had bent them a little to peep inside some of the rooms when no one was looking. He had been told that he would find the King's shoes in an anteroom just off the George IV suite and, to be sure, he made no noise that might disturb the royal guest. He opened the door quietly and bent down to pick up the shoes. As he did so, the door to the royal bedchamber opened and a servant in a smart grey livery came out leading a small wire-haired terrier. At once it began to pull towards George, wagging its tail furiously. Automatically George bent down to stroke it.

'Oh, he can stand any amount of that kind of treatment,' the servant said with a smile. 'He's as spoilt as he can be.'

George continued to fondle the dog's ears, and as he did so he took note of the handsome silver collar which bore the inscription: 'My name is Caesar. I belong to the King.' It was a very brief encounter for the next minute the servant was off down the corridor at a brisk pace to take Caesar for his morning run. But George was jubilant. He had actually stroked the King's pet and everyone knew how fond His Majesty was of the terrier, which was even allowed to sleep on the foot of his royal master's bed. He couldn't wait to tell his brother about the incident next time they met.

He was a bit disappointed in the King's footwear. He didn't really know what he had expected royal shoes to be like, but they seemed to be an ordinary pair of patent leather, just like anyone else's.

All that week the lavish entertaining continued. During the day Lord and Lady Savile and the King and his party were away at the race course, so the staff were able to proceed with their normal duties at a reasonable speed. However, in the evening, once the family and guests were home, the pace became as furious as ever until after midnight. Only once that week did George catch a glimpse of the King, walking in the rose gardens, with his little dog at his heels, chatting with Mrs Keppel. He saw this little scene by chance through a small pantry window

that partly overlooked the gardens, and even then he had
to stand on a chair to do so. The King stopped to admire a
certain rose and George had to smile as he noticed what
Caesar thought of another as he lifted his leg against the
bush. He wondered what his brother would have said if
he had seen the incident. Arthur wouldn't have been
amused, whether it was the King's dog or not.

The frantic week came to a close as King Edward and
his entourage left Rufford with the same pomp and
ceremony that had greeted his arrival. The entire staff had
shared in the excitement and were justly proud of their
efforts. Yet, as the carriages disappeared from view down
the drive, everyone gave a sigh of relief. The royal visit
had been a success and now they could get back to normal
for a little while, at least until Rufford Abbey began to
prepare for Christmas.

George and his brother were fortunate in both being
given Christmas leave that year and snow fell in time for
the festive period. The family celebrations at Babworth
were especially happy, but all too soon it was over and
the boys were setting out on bicycles on their return to
Rufford. It was about eight miles along snowy lanes and,
in some places, it was difficult to stay on their wheels, but
even this proved a source of fun to the two brothers.

Rufford looked beautiful under a mantle of snow, and
the double avenue of lime trees appeared as if it had
suddenly burst into blossom. A blizzard during the night
had coated every twig, and the sun glinted on the snow-
covered Abbey. Inside, the house was still festive, with
large twisted garlands of scarlet holly and evergreens,
and even the old crypt, or servants' hall, was decorated
with paper streamers, balloons and Christmas rings. The
staff who had not been home for the period had apparently had a wonderful time.

It was a tradition at Rufford Abbey that protocol was

relaxed over the Christmas period. All the servants, regardless of rank, were allowed to mix freely at this time. Even the little scullery maids were able to join the others. The traditional Christmas dinner was always taken at midday, and instead of the lower staff waiting, as usual, on the above stairs staff, the footmen and the butler on this occasion served the underlings. It was all performed with lots of fun and leg-pulling that would never have been permitted at any other time of year.

New Year's Eve provided another rather special event at Rufford. There was always a grand ball, with hundreds of high society guests to see the old year out in great style. The servants were also allowed to celebrate by organising their own ball in the old crypt. For a few hours, all members of the staff could mix again and even dance with one another. Then, sometime during the evening, Lord and Lady Savile would look in for half an hour to wish them all a happy new year, and quite often would join in the fun. This might be the only time that certain members of the kitchen staff ever saw the owners of Rufford Abbey from one year to the next. It was rather odd to see Her Ladyship allowing herself to be waltzed round by one of her footmen, and His Lordship partnering a pretty parlour maid. George had the time of his life, for he had discovered that he had an aptitude for dancing. At the first chimes of midnight tankards were raised in salute to the new year; then, as everyone linked arms to sing 'Auld lang syne' under the large oil lamps and gay decorations, the old year came to an end. One minute all were equal, from the housekeeper down to the lowest scullery maid, and the next it was back to their own departments.

⮾ 5 ⮾
The Perils of
London Town

It was 1905, and George was nearing his seventeenth
year. He had been in service as a member of the inside
staff for two years and, although he was well estab-
lished as head hall boy, he began to feel restless. He had
heard it said that if a servant failed to climb above stairs
before the age of twenty he was destined to remain a
lower-class servant all his life. George didn't intend this
to happen if he could help it, but good references were
needed to climb those stairs and the only way to get them
was to seek further experience in a higher position elsewhere. It had to be done step by step; there was no short
cut to success in this profession.

George had not *wanted* to leave the services of Lord
Savile, for he had been very happy there, but his chances
of any real promotion were remote. Rather than promote

lower-grade servants to above-stairs level, it was considered preferable to bring in someone from outside, mainly because it was almost impossible for a newly promoted person to hold his social standing with others of lower grade with whom he had previously worked. The most George could hope for at Rufford Abbey was a slightly higher position in top pantry, but he had his sights set on much better things. The only thing to do was to move on.

He mentioned his thoughts to his brother the next time they met for a drink and asked his opinion. Arthur wasn't able to give much advice, for he himself had no such ambitions. He was satisfied to stay in the gardening profession, where he would move up the ladder automatically as the older men retired. He loved his work and nothing would have induced him to go changing his job at every touch and turn. All he was really able to do was to encourage his brother to go after whatever it was he wanted and to wish him luck.

George talked with enthusiasm of the things he had heard about London, the big city which had become like a will-o-the-wisp to a young man with ambitions. He had seen pictures of the aristocracy at royal garden parties at Buckingham Palace and Windsor Castle, the red carpet rolled out and elegant footmen in close attendance. This is what he wanted. He had no intention of staying among the pots and pans and to be scrubbing black-lead from his nails all his life. He decided that the sooner he started the sooner that day would come.

On his next day off he went along to the nearest agency for domestic service, one of the best in the Midlands, and asked them to enter his name on their lists for any position above stairs. Impressed that he was already in service to Rufford Abbey, they accepted his application without more ado. He was told he would be notified as soon as there was a vacancy and he came away feeling he had done the right thing.

Two months went by. He began to think they had forgotten him, or had decided that he was too young for the leap above stairs. Then, just as he was becoming resigned to waiting perhaps another year, a letter arrived. It simply said that a post they thought might interest him had become vacant, and requested him to contact them at his earliest possible convenience. He went along to the agency with wings on his feet and was informed that there was a vacancy for a junior footman at Brittwell Court, Burnham Beeches, the home of a certain Mr Christie Miller. He was a little bit disappointed that the gentleman was not a titled personage; however, the job was right, and the salary was more than satisfactory. When he told the housekeeper his news, she expressed her pleasure at his good fortune in having the chance to better himself while so young; but she also warned him that there would be strong competition for the post and that he shouldn't be disappointed if he was not chosen this time. She wished him luck and added that she would be sorry to lose him from the staff.

George spent the days before his interview in a state of half excitement, half apprehension. He had never travelled further than the nearest town of Worksop; now here he was about to take his first trip to London.

Arthur, who came to see him off from Retford station, appeared much more cheerful than he actually felt. He was secretly a little fearful for his brother's safety in the big city and he also felt sad that it was taking George away from him.

'You keep a tight hold on that hat, our George, or someone might pinch it!' was Arthur's parting shot as the train pulled out.

The hat was a bowler, which George had bought especially for the interview. It suited him very well, but the first time Arthur had seen him wear it he had gone into fits of laughter. Now, as the train gathered speed, George waved it from the carriage window. Then he settled back to watch the countryside flash by. At one time the train went so fast that it rocked on its metal track and he began to feel most uneasy. He hoped his alarm didn't show itself to the other passengers. He tried to keep his mind occupied with the coming interview, but this was almost as disturbing. He wondered, for instance, what Mr Christie Miller would think of his Midlands accent. It was not very pronounced because he had tried carefully to modify it during the time he worked at Rufford, realising it was necessary if he wished eventually to aspire to the level of personal servant. He had practised forming his words properly, using correct English. He was not a conceited young man, otherwise he would not have worried over such trifles. He had yet to learn that he possessed physical assets which would make up for his accent and appeal to the rich and fashionable employers. They preferred their personal staff to look good in every aspect, often to the point of matching them in height and build. George was five foot eleven, and handsome too; if only he had known this at the time, he wouldn't have had a qualm in the world.

As the train rushed on, the green countryside began to give way to shunting yards, huge warehouses and tall, blackened buildings. It was a sight very far removed from his mental picture of London. King's Cross was dirty and dismal, and he began to feel he must have boarded the wrong train. He stepped out on to the platform feeling bewildered and nervous. Several huge engines belched forth steam. Their noise echoed under the great canopy of steel and glass and their shrill whistles pierced his eardrums. Station wagons, piled high with luggage, rattled and wove their way at great speed through equally fast-moving crowds. George had to jump clear as one came bearing down on him; all this

turmoil was deafening to a boy whose ears were tuned
only to the sounds of nature. He had the strongest desire
to leap back on the next train to Retford, but took refuge
in a comparatively quiet corner to compose himself for
the next step. He stared in amazement as people rushed
about in all directions as if their lives depended on it.
He would have asked someone how to get out of this
enormous station if only there had been someone who
looked as though he had a moment to spare. After a
while, he realised there was no sense in just standing
there. Taking a deep breath, he plunged into the crowd
and managed to get a porter to stand still long enough to
ask him the way to the cab rank. Even then, all he got was
a quick jerk of the man's thumb in the right direction
before he pelted up the platform. He struggled through
the barrier and found the horse-drawn cabs just outside
the station. After giving the 'cabby' the address he
wanted in Sloane Square, he got in and they started up the
cobbled ramp and out into the street.

Poor George! If he had thought it bad in the station, it
was nothing to what he encountered as soon as they left
the station yard. Never had he seen such a confusion of
vehicles, all going in different directions – it seemed a
miracle they didn't end up in a heap in the middle. Horse-
drawn buses emblazoned with adverts for Bryant & May
matches, Johnny Walker whisky or Sloan's liniment,
jostled alongside brightly painted coster carts. Even
the broughams and landaus, drawn by high-stepping
thoroughbreds, fought it out for road space, often with
only inches to spare. George had seen these elegant
carriages before, but only when they came in stately
procession up the drive of Rufford Abbey. He hadn't
expected to see them in a free for all like this.

He sat gripping the edge of his seat, thinking every
moment they would collide. The cabby must have seen
the concern on George's face through the mirror at the

top of the cab, for he called down to him.

'Don't fret, guv, I ain't never lorst a passenger yet.'

George thought how curious his cockney accent was, but it served to calm him a little as they progressed into the West End. In this part of London things were very different and interest began to take over from his nervousness. Smart shop windows displayed only the very best of everything and there were prosperous-looking people everywhere. Even the traffic was more orderly and it looked much more like the London he had imagined. Now that the cab had stopped playing catch-me-if-you-can with everything else in the road, he could have happily ridden round all day just taking it all in.

' 'Ere y'ar, guv, safe and sarnd,' the driver joked cheerfully, as he brought the cab to a halt outside the smart-looking agency.

Everything inside was very luxurious, with a décor of white and gold, and thick pile carpets on the floor. George handed his introduction card to an important-looking person, who spoke as though he had a plum in his mouth.

'Will you please take a seat, sir?'

George had never been called 'sir' before, and it made him feel like royalty. He sat down, twisting his hat nervously, wondering how long it would be before he was called. Within the next half hour other well-dressed young men began to arrive, until there were sixteen of them, all apparently waiting to be interviewed for the same job. They sat eyeing one another discreetly, and in complete silence. Not so much as a smile passed between them and this began to get on George's nerves. He decided to break the ice by speaking to the young man sitting next to him and was greeted by blank astonishment. When the young man did reply, it was as briefly as possible and in such a refined voice that George began to wonder if his journey had been a waste of time.

At last the interviewing began. Applicants were called in alphabetical order. This meant that George was near the end of the list. As each one went in, the others continued to eye one another or to stare fixedly at the opposite wall. As each one came out, George tried to read his expression, but in his deflated mind they all seemed to look confident.

It was over an hour before he heard his name called, and he rose stiffly. Sitting on the hard edge of his chair for so long had given him pins and needles in his legs, but he forced himself to walk to the door with as much nonchalance as he could muster.

The room he entered was quite small and seemed to be dominated by a large desk, behind which sat a distinguished-looking gentleman, presumably Mr Christie Miller. He smiled and invited George to sit down. Although he seemed only to glance at him casually from time to time, George knew that not a single detail of his appearance would escape him by the time the interview was over.

An official made the introductions, after which George sat silently while Mr Christie Miller scrutinised the reference in front of him. Then came the questions and George was surprised how very well he was able to answer them. He only elaborated when it seemed necessary to do so; otherwise he answered as briefly as possible. He felt so much at ease that he even forgot about his accent. As the interview came to an end, Mr Christie Miller smiled once more and said he would be notified. George went back to his chair in the vestibule.

Only one other applicant remained, a tall, willowy young man. His interview lasted about fifteen minutes, though to George it seemed an eternity. When he emerged, George, to his utter astonishment, heard his name called a second time. He went in and heard almost in a dream that he had been chosen for the post. He would join the staff of Brittwell Court in one month's time. With this, Mr Christie Miller shook hands with him and George left the agency on top of the world.

Outside on the pavement again, George looked round for a cab and, by sheer chance, saw the same jovial-faced cabby who had brought him from the station.

' 'Ow djer get on, mate?' This was almost the first friendly word he had heard since he had arrived in London.

'I was lucky, I got the job, but how did you know?'

The cabby grinned. 'Easy, mate. I sees 'em all in my job, an' I knows a gentleman's gent when I sees one. Got it stamped all over you, you'av.'

The cab began its journey back to the station, weaving in and out of the traffic at the same breakneck speed, but this time George was too busy with his thoughts to worry about it. He paid the cabby off (plus a tip) at King's Cross and was about to enter the station when a strange young woman approached him. She was about his own age and quite pretty, although very heavily made up, and wore a feather boa at a jaunty angle over her shoulders. She laid a gloved hand on George's arm and gave him a dimpled smile.

'You're a handsome young gent,' she said. ' 'Ow would you like t'buy me a nice cuppa tea?'

To say that George was surprised would be an understatement. The girl was a stranger and girls from his own town didn't behave like this. At first he was lost for words. He didn't want to be unfriendly, but there was something about her that made him feel uneasy. He explained politely that he had to catch a train almost at once, otherwise he would be delighted to buy her some tea and then he began to move away.

'Ah, come on guv, you ain't that green, an' a girl's got to earn a livin', yer know,' she persisted.

Well, that was where she was wrong; George *was* still

very green about such things. He had never before met this situation, nor this type of girl. The cabby saw his predicament and came to his aid. In plain cockney language, he told her to clear off. She in turn flew at him, spitting fire and brimstone and using words one would scarcely hear in a barrack room. However, to George's relief, she went. He didn't understand it, but his sense of chivalry made him feel he should say something in the girl's defence, and he told the cabby he thought he had been hard on her.

'She didn't seem a bad sort of girl, perhaps she really couldn't afford to buy tea.'

The cabby roared with laughter. 'Blimey, mate, you've got a lot t'learn. She ain't no nice gel, guv. She's the biggest ole Tom round 'ere fer miles.'

Once aboard his train the incident was shelved in George's mind, to be replaced by thoughts of new clothes he should have to start his new job.

He was back at Rufford in time to meet his brother at the local, as they had arranged before he left. There were a few other members of the Rufford staff present and they were all very interested in the account of George's day. There was an uproar when he came to the episode of the strange young lady with the painted face. Arthur, just as astonished as George had been, was astounded at the cabby's treatment of her and that he had called her an 'old Tom'.

'They must be a queer lot oop theer, George,' he said. 'I've niver 'eard of a girl being called Tom before. They'll want a bit o' gettin' used to.'

By now, the older men were in fits of laughter, and they decided it was time to enlighten the two lads, who were obviously ignorant of the facts of life. They explained just what a prostitute was, and that the slang name for such women was 'old Tom', which tickled Arthur's sense of humour.

'Crikey, our George! It didn't tek you long t'get in hot water, did it? You'll 'av t'watch yerself, lad, or we'll be readin' about you in't Sunday papers.'

The next day George went to see the housekeeper to hand in his notice. At once this rather austere woman dropped her reserve long enough to congratulate him on being chosen for a job that required a great deal more than the ability to use a black-lead brush.

His parents took the news calmly, but George felt they had grave doubts about the wisdom of such a move. However, they were beginning to realise that their son was an ambitious young man, determined to reach the top as soon as he could and in the face of this they felt it would be wrong to stand in his way. George himself had the occasional worry about how he would cope with this new and more responsible situation, but he said nothing to his parents, nor indeed to anyone else. The deed was done and he just had to do well.

He went to a young gentleman's outfitters and ordered two suits, one in black and another in navy. These, together with two white shirts and a couple of conservative ties, used up almost all his savings. However, he felt it to be a good investment. His wage as hall boy of eight shillings a week was leaping up to thirty shillings a week as a footman and – for a boy of George's age – this was more than just good, it was splendid. He would be able to put back the money he had carefully saved in no time, he thought. What he didn't take into account was the much higher cost of living in a smart county like Buckinghamshire.

～ 6 ～
Footman in Ireland

B rittwell Court seemed very small indeed compared
with the enormous estate George had just left.
Even the main rooms, which were a fair size, were
smaller than Rufford Abbey's vineries. The staff, twenty-
nine in all, consisted of cook and a dozen or so kitchen
staff, a hall boy, four in the pantry, butler, housekeeper,
two chamber maids, two parlour maids, valet, lady's
maid and three footmen. However, George discovered
that protocol was observed here as anywhere else, and the
Christie Millers did a lot of entertaining. If the guest lists
did not include royalty, they were still very influential
people who came to Brittwell Court.

George was received and shown to the footmen's
rooms. He was given a temporary livery – worn by his
predecessor who must have been roughly the same size

because it wasn't a bad fit – and was informed that a new livery would be tailored for him in due course. Then came his first introduction to dressing for dinner. The other two footmen were decent chaps willing to familiarise him with his duties. Powdering the hair was the difficult part and the first time George tried this the others almost went into hysterics. Wigs had not yet become accepted as part of the footman's ceremonial regalia, and so this complicated and lengthy procedure had to be mastered in order to make the natural hair resemble a wig.

First the hair had to be soaked in warm water, as if it were about to be washed, and soft soap was applied and worked into a thick lather. Sweet smelling violet powder was then sprinkled on with a large powder puff until the whole head was coated. After that the hair was combed in the usual way and the surplus scraped off round the edges with a wooden spatula, leaving the finished result looking exactly like a white wig. It had to be done right the first time, because it dried out quickly, as hard as plaster of Paris. Failure meant at least twenty minutes' soaking the stiffened hair in hot water before it could be washed out again and dinner couldn't be held up for the process to be repeated. George had to put in some practice before he got the knack.

He also had to learn to keep his own livery smart, for these elaborate garments were only cleaned professionally twice a year, and it would never have done for him to appear with his doeskin breeches less than immaculate. Apart from the breeches, the livery consisted of a black velvet waistcoat, white lawn shirt with lace cravat, long silk stockings, black shoes with silver buckles, and a maroon tail coat with a tall Byron collar. When he looked in the mirror, he could hardly believe his own reflection and smiled at the thought of what his brother would say to see him in this regalia.

46

George had been well drilled by his colleagues in the way dinner had to be served, but he still felt fearful that something might go wrong. The first footman, who was the senior in status, served at 'top table', which was reserved for the family and the most important among the dinner guests. The second footman served to the right and the third to the left. In this way there was no confusion and the diners were served more or less at the same time.

In fact, George's début as a footman went without a hitch. He neither fell flat on his face, nor dropped anything on the floor and he was soon able to take it all in his stride. He settled into the household, which was just as friendly as Rufford. The only difference was that his friends were above stairs and he was not allowed to associate too closely with those below his station.

Then came the first real adventure of his life in gentleman's service. After two months at Brittwell Court, the family started to pack up and the whole household prepared to move to the Christie Millers' estate in Ireland for the summer vacation. As George had never so much as rowed himself across Babworth Lake, the prospect of crossing the Irish Sea was both disturbing and exciting.

Although he did not yet realise it, certain changes were taking place in him. In the time since he had left home he had begun to acquire a more independent outlook on life and a polish which he hadn't possessed before. Even his accent was now less pronounced. He was more able to cope with situations that before would have started an army of butterflies doing battle in the pit of his stomach.

When the day of departure came, dust sheets were draped over the furniture and the house was closed up. The staff, with the exception of the valet, the lady's maid and the three footmen, were packed off to board the Fishguard train by their own devices, while the family

47

travelled to the station by carriages with the footmen in attendance. George rode with the last carriage, sitting high up on the 'dicky seat' at the back. He was wearing his outdoor livery, a smart ensemble in dark chocolate brown, with yards of gold braid and buttons, a rolled brim 'topper' with a cockade and smart leather gloves. He couldn't help noticing how eyes turned to watch them go by, though it was not an uncommon sight, for most people of quality travelled this way, the ladies with their elaborate hats and frivolous little silk parasols to hide their delicate complexions from the sun, the gentlemen sitting erect and looking important; the horses, with coats groomed until they shone like silk.

At Fishguard the second footman unfortunately became ill with appendicitis and had to be rushed to hospital. Otherwise, the crossing was uneventful, and George wasn't sick, as he feared he might be. From Waterford they travelled to the Christie Millers' country residence near Limerick. It was a comparatively small but beautiful house. Large, low windows overlooked velvety lawns and gardens ablaze with summer flowers. Huge pedestal basins and urns filled with the same riot of colour stood at the foot of a graceful flight of stone steps that led to the front entrance. To the back of the house, tennis courts and long herbaceous borders stretched down to a row of old willow trees dipping their green trails in the waters of the river Shannon.

As soon as they arrived Mr Christie Miller telephoned an agency in Cork for a replacement for his sick footman. However, they were unable to offer the same high qualifications as the Regina Bureau in London, but the man who was sent was highly recommended to their standards. He arrived the next day and for a time things ran smoothly, for he obviously knew his duties well. He was a likeable chap who got on with the other staff and was always ready with a joke. It was soon clear, however, that he had one rather serious flaw in his character: he drank too much. Nearly all his free time was spent at the nearest pub and he would arrive back flushed, tongue-tied and sometimes unsteady on his feet. At first, the other staff were amused and thought him to be quite a lad, but as he went on returning a little later each time, George and his colleagues became tired of covering up for him. Indeed, it was quite often difficult to sober him up into a fit state to serve dinner. They tried to tell him how foolish it was to jeopardise a good position by this over-indulgence, but he only laughed and told them, 'You worry too much.'

Two days before an important dinner party, Mr Christie Miller had to go away on business and so the footmen were comparatively free until he returned. The weather was glorious and George spent his time with rod and line on the banks of the Shannon. The first footman had made the acquaintance of a pretty Irish girl, and he spent most of his free time with her. The new footman, of course, spent his time in the pubs, which at this time were open from dawn till dusk.

As Mr Christie Miller wasn't due back until the next day, they weren't particularly worried when the erring footman failed to return that night; but when he didn't appear the next morning, they began to be anxious. Dinner that evening was scheduled for eight o'clock sharp, and some important people were expected. They knew that two footmen could never cope adequately; certainly not without 'the boss' noticing that the new footman was missing.

As the day wore on, they anxiously watched the clock. Then at two o'clock in the afternoon a donkey-cart rattled up the drive to the back door, with several high-spirited Irishmen kicking up a hell of a row. George and his fellow footman went out to see what all the shouting was about, just in time to see the missing footman dumped unceremoniously on the doorstep. After loud laughter and lusty farewells, the rest of the unruly party drove off. The noise they made was enough to rouse the dead. The erring footman was hustled quickly into the house before anyone else became curious. He was quite unable to stand, so they half-carried, half-dragged him up the back stairs to the footmen's quarters and there tried to revive him. He stank of liquor and, judging by the state of his clothes, must have spent the night in a pig-sty. They stripped him off and dumped him into a tepid bath, hoping it would have a sobering effect. All it succeeded in doing was to draw forth a stream of obscene language, while the man remained hopelessly drunk. Next they tried black coffee, but this too failed to have effect. Someone suggested a strong dose of bicarbonate of soda, which certainly worked as an emetic, but did little to bring the stupid man to his senses. They walked him round and round the room, but after an hour of this treatment, his legs were still like jelly. The only thing left was to put him to bed and hope he would sleep it off.

As explained, dressing for dinner took all of two hours, even for the most experienced footman, so they could only allow the man to sleep until six at the very latest. They covered him with an eiderdown, and hoped that it would do the trick. They peeped in from time to time to see if there was any sign of him coming round, but he snored on, filling the room with alcoholic fumes from his breath. The first footman declared that if someone struck a match the roof would blow off. At six o'clock they pulled him out of bed and walked him round the room again. This time they were at least able to get him to stand up on his own, but he still couldn't speak without getting his tongue in a knot. As they washed and powdered his hair, it was like handling a rag doll, and they could only hope that sheer instinct would carry him through dinner without disaster.

The dinner gong sounded and the guests assembled at the dinner table. It was time for the footmen to begin their regal walk into the dining room with the large tureens of piping hot consommé. The first footman took the lead to the top table with the tureen held breast-high in true ceremonial fashion. Then it was the second footman's turn to follow to the right-hand side of the table. George pointed him in the right direction and hoped for the best. He set off on a zig-zag path, with one garter hanging round his ankle. George noticed with horror that in their haste to get him dressed they had buttoned his jacket into the wrong holes. However, the guests seemed too engrossed in conversation to notice his untidy appearance and, to George's relief, he served the first guest without mishap.

It was now George's turn to carry in his tureen to the left of the table. As he did so, he could see his drunken colleague heading straight for the up-raised head of a lion-skin rug. Helpless to do anything, he watched the second footman miss it by inches; but as he made his way back there was a terrible crash. The lid of the tureen smashed to pieces on the floor, and the hot consommé was thrown right down the front of Mr Christie Miller's dress suit.

The guests leapt to their feet and pandemonium broke out. To make matters worse, the erring footman lay on his back on the floor with a silly grin on his face. Had it been a genuine accident, however bad, it could have been excused; but one sniff of the man's breath and the 'boss' went mad. It was instant dismissal. He was carted from the dining room by the other footmen, while Mr Christie Miller went to change. Meanwhile, the chef stormed and raved in the kitchen because his carefully prepared meal was spoiling.

The next morning the Irish footman was sent packing with a considerable hang-over and without a reference.

George and his colleague were informed that they were expected to cope until the family were back in London, where a more reliable replacement would be found. They didn't find this too difficult because the entertaining was kept down to a minimum. Apart from feeling sorry that the other man's career was clearly finished, they were relieved that no more covering-up would have to be done.

As the weather remained perfect, George took to roaming the country lanes on his free afternoons. On one such lovely afternoon he walked along the downs and discovered that shamrocks really did grow everywhere. Picking a sprig for his lapel, he followed a foot-path that eventually brought him out on to a road where he saw an old man sunning himself on a low wall.

'Good afternoon sur-r-r-, t'is a lovely day, and thanks be t'God that we're all aloive t'see it.'

George returned his greeting, and the old man went on:

'Will yer stop awhile, an' refresh yerself now? T'is a hot day, so it is.'

The old man's deeply lined face beamed at the prospect of someone to chat to, and he led the way into his cottage. As soon as George's eyes became accustomed to the gloom, he was appalled by the filth and squalor. There was only one room, with a bare earth floor. Chickens and other animals came in and out as they pleased, while the largest pig he had ever seen lay full-length in front of the peat fire which burned in a scooped-out hollow in the ground, lined with stones, over which a metal cowl drew the thick smoke out through a hole in the roof. A rough wooden table was set under the single window, which was so dirty that it was impossible to see out. A pile of rags in a far corner obviously served the old man as a bed.

He indicated a seat and then offered George a tin mug

of homemade ginger-beer. George looked ruefully at the chipped and dirty container, and surreptitiously rubbed the rim with his cuff before putting it to his mouth. He wouldn't have insulted his host for the world, but he was willing to bet that mug hadn't seen water for months. However, the drink was refreshing as he sat listening to the old man talking. During their conversation, George remarked on the pig lying in front of the fire.

'Does he always hog the fire like that?'

His host looked at him in astonishment. 'An' who's more a roit t'the fire than the feller who pays the rent?'

George felt there was no answer to that and changed the subject.

In their free time George and the first footman found much to do together. They shared the same sense of humour and had many things in common. There was, however, one pastime they didn't share and that was swimming. The first footman was an excellent swimmer, but George was unable to swim a stroke. While his companion splashed about in the water, George would sit on the bank and look after his clothes. The weather was still very hot and George often envied the other man his obvious enjoyment in the cool of the water. George would explain that he had never learned to swim, chiefly on account of the tragedy of his elder brother's drowning. His colleague understood this, but reasoned that he himself held a life-saving certificate and that little harm could come to George with a pair of water-wings. George eventually gave in and decided to risk it.

With a packed lunch-box they set off to find a secluded spot on the river bank some distance from the house, because neither man possessed a bathing suit. When they found a sufficiently private place, the other footman swam out into the wide river, kicking and splashing, while George dabbled with his water-wings nearer the bank.

The water was cool and George began to think there was a lot to be said for bathing – so long as he was able to touch the bottom. Suddenly there was a shout from the footman out in mid-stream and George saw that he was pointing to a bulky object with horns that was floating along in the water. Somewhat alarmed, both men left the water quickly and clambered to the highest part of the bank where they could watch in safety. Whatever it was, it didn't seem to be very active, so the first footman decided to investigate. It turned out to be a cow and he towed it into the bank, not knowing for sure if the poor creature was dead or not. Once in shallow water, they were very soon aware that it was not only dead, but that it had been so for some long time. The stench was awful. Bathing seemed to lose its charm after that.

Returning to the place where they had left their clothes, they found to their consternation that everything had vanished. Frantically they searched up and down the bank, but could only conclude that their garments had been stolen. It was an awkward predicament, for they hadn't so much as a towel between them. As they were about three miles from the house, they set about gathering some of the bracken that grew in abundance along the river bank and then, clutching one bunch in front and another behind, they started for home, hoping that they wouldn't encounter anyone on the way. The journey was a nightmare. Stones cut into their feet, and several times they had to jump in a ditch or over the nearest hedge when they heard voices. One of these leaps ended in a patch of nettles and they had to continue their furtive way home with the added indignity of blisters on their backsides. They also discovered that gorse had a habit of shedding its spines, which became uncomfortably embedded in the soles of their feet.

It was with genuine relief that eventually they reached the grounds of the house – only to realise that their troubles were not yet over. The gardens stretched down to the water's edge, and to reach the back of the house they would have to cross a wide expanse of lawns, over-looked by the large drawing-room windows.

As they crouched in the shrubbery, racking their brains to think what to do, an old gardener appeared round the corner of the house. George and his companion whistled to attract the old man's attention. At first he simply stood and looked around him, wondering where the whistle came from. George waved one naked arm from the cover of the bushes, and this caught the man's eye. But garden-ers, like the things they grow, never do things in a hurry and this one was no exception. He ambled across in his own good time and peered at the two naked footmen as though he didn't believe his own eyes. George quickly explained how their clothes had been stolen and they had to wait a few more precious minutes while the old chap had a fit of near hysterics at their predicament. When he recovered, he agreed to help them by giving a signal when the coast was clear. Then he walked slowly back to the house, under the pretence of pulling up a few weeds in the flower beds, and peered through the windows to make sure the rooms were empty.

At the given signal, the two footmen ran like mad things across the lawns to the side of the house. Once round the corner, they would be fairly safe. They made a bee-line for the back stairs and the privacy of their own rooms. But at the top of the stairs came their biggest shock – the sight of their clothes arranged in a neat pile! Standing nearby were the two nurse-maids, laughing their silly heads off. They had taken the children out in the donkey-cart during the afternoon, had seen the two men bathing, and decided to take their clothes for a bit of a lark.

'That will teach you to go bathing in the rude,' one girl giggled.

They were most surprised when the men failed to see the joke.

'Don't be a couple of old bears. We were only testing your initiative,' said the other.

Looking back on the incident, George agreed that the situation must have had its funny side to anyone who didn't have to endure it. But at the time he felt it was a good thing Mr Christie Miller insisted on his staff having even dispositions, otherwise he might have had to get himself two new nurse-maids.

One fine afternoon, George stopped to speak to a man who was cutting the lawns with a horse-drawn mower. After their conversation had progressed a while, 'Paddy' invited George to attend a wake. George had never heard the word 'wake', but decided it must be a village gathering of some kind and accepted.

'If ye be wantin' t'meet the village folk, an' 'av a real good toim, then you cum-a-long-o-me tomorra,' Paddy told him.

George asked him how he should dress for this important event, to which Paddy replied, 'Oh! just come as ye-are moi friend, an' take pot luck wi' the rest of us.'

So, at two o'clock on the following afternoon, dressed in a plain suit with a conservative tie, George presented himself at the village inn. He could hear the sound of laughter before he got there. Ducking his head under the low beams, he entered the small bar, where it seemed the whole of the male population were gathered. Paddy spotted him at once and came to greet him. He led George over to the counter and made the most of showing him off.

' 'E lives wi them foin peeple in the big house, an he's come t'drink wid us. Now what d'yere tink o'that?' he said.

A tankard was pushed into George's hand and, although it was evident they were all well soaked in the strong porter, the heavy drinking went on for another hour. Then, just as George had resigned himself to the thought that a 'wake' must be another name for a good booze-up, the party began to move.

He followed the long line of Irishmen, who for some reason walked one behind the other, out of the door and down the village street. The fresh air was welcome after the fug of cigarettes and peat smoke. Led by the village priest, they entered a cottage, where women were laying out sandwiches and turning griddle cakes on the stove. There were large jugs of porter standing on every flat surface in the small room. An old man sat with his bare feet in the hearth, playing a lively jig on a concertina. Their tankards filled yet again, everyone began to dance. George decided it must be someone's birthday party. He let his eyes travel round that poor little room, with its rough furniture and its air of dilapidation. Then the hairs on the back of his neck began to bristle as his eye alighted on a coffin standing up on its end, the lid drawn half-way down to show the corpse inside. At that moment, Paddy appeared at his elbow, linking his arm through George's.

'Now – will ye come away an' pay yere respects to me auld grannie? God bless 'er.'

He led George over to the upturned coffin, where he raised his tankard and wished the old girl a happy journey. Then George watched, horrified, as one after another saluted the corpse. They were all blind drunk by this time. One man tried to feed some of the contents of his tankard through the stiff lips. The man with the concertina played for all he was worth, while the bereaved chanted 'Oh, sure, why did yer die, look what yere missin', why did yer die?'

It shocked George to the core, and he could always recall that parchment-like face, with the straggly wisps of grey hair. He wished he could escape from this macabre ritual. Eventually the coffin lid was closed. With great difficulty, six men hoisted the coffin on to their shoulders and, led by the priest swinging incense, they started down the village street. The womenfolk waved them off, mopping their eyes on their aprons. They apparently didn't attend funerals.

Between the uneven cobblestones and the fact that the bearers were of different heights, George quite expected to see the unfortunate grandmother tipped out on to the street. When they came to the pub where the party had begun, they propped the coffin across a horse trough and made for the bar. This was too much for George, and he caught Paddy's arm.

'You're surely not going to leave her out here, are you?' he asked.

The little Irishman turned a surprised face. 'An' where d'yere tink she'll be goin' to, all by 'erself?' he replied.

Another hour was spent drinking hard, with the village priest keeping pace with the rest. Then again they hoisted the coffin on to their shoulders and tottered and swayed with it up the stone steps to the cemetery, where at last, to George's relief, the old lady was laid to her rest.

During that visit George discovered that Ireland was a place of many strange customs and superstitions. They were intensely religious and yet they used lucky charms to ward off evil spirits. They would share their last crust with you one minute and beat your brains out with a shillelagh the next, but George got on with them very well.

On one of his afternoon walks, he encountered a woman sitting outside her cottage, making the most beautiful lace. After passing the time of day, he remarked to her on the intricate patterns of the lace. She told him they were passed down through generations by memory only, and that each pattern told a story. He asked if he might buy some and, because George was generous with payment, she offered to tell his fortune.

He waited, then she began.

She made a pot of strong tea and, after draining the leaves, she took George's cup and looked into it.

'You've a lucky face, sur-r, but let's see what the leaves have to say.'

'You're a gud livin' man, so ye're, an' yer loves yer family, specially yer mother. You've a young woman who is waitin' t'be with yer, an' she's one of a big family.'

This was true, but George felt it to be rather a stock prediction that could fit anyone.

'You're a lucky young fella, but ye won't always be as well off as y'are now. Y'll meet a few very 'ard toimes in yer loife, Oi c'n see roughs as well as smooths.'

'Can you be more specific about these?' George prompted. She gazed into the cup quietly for a moment, then set it down and looked earnestly at him.

'The leaves aren't always specific, sur-r, but for the immediate future, you will travel far and see wonderful things. You will come back to Ireland sur-r, but when ye do, it will be under very distressing circumstances.'

It made no sense at the time, but George had reason to recall the lace-maker's words later in his career.

7

Butler at Eighteen

The Christie Millers returned to Brittwell Court at the end of September, by which time George had been in their service for six months and was entitled to his first leave of absence. Naturally his destination was Babworth, and he arrived home to a very enthusiastic welcome. His mother apparently had not known a good night's sleep all the time he had been in Ireland, fearful for his safety when crossing that expanse of water. In her relief to see him back, George found himself nearly hugged to death and later that same evening, when he joined his friends at the local, he was the centre of attraction to so many eager to hear all about his visit to this other country. To George it was like old times; nothing seemed to have changed. But his friends, lads he had known all his life, noticed a difference in him.

60

He no longer spoke bluntly, but with a certain refine-
ment; he even had a trace of southern accent which
marked him out as different. He could now afford good
clothes of style and cut that were out of place in a country
village, where most young men wore cloth caps and
boots. He went to drink in his best suit simply because he
no longer owned anything else; but even his brother
Arthur confided to their parents, 'By gum! Our George is
turning into a toff. I 'ope 'ee doesn't out-grow us.'

During his leave the Whitakers held their annual shoot.
George joined the men on the estate who were enrolled as
beaters, and it was while they were taking refreshment
that he met young 'Jackie' Whitaker again after a number
of years. George had grown up with the young master
and, although he could never claim to have been a playmate, there had been times when 'Jackie' had escaped the
attentions of 'Nanny' to enjoy a game. Since then, of
course, their paths had diverged, but strangely enough
they still seemed to find a lot to say to each other. They
laughed and joked together while they drank cider and
tucked into the assortment of sandwiches. Some of the
men of the estate, who still held the gentry in awe, were
surprised to hear them conversing apparently on equal
terms. While working in close contact with upper-class
people, George had discovered they were quite human,
and he no longer harboured feelings of inferiority. Even
his own brother was a little horrified to hear George
explain quite openly, but politely, that he thought it was
wrong to kill for fun. Master Jack had brought the subject
up by asking why George was not with the guns that day
and George told him truthfully that he preferred to see
the birds sitting along the garden fence.

'I'll bet it's because you're a rotten shot,' Jackie
laughed.

There was another surprise when Sir Albert Whitaker
came to thank and pay off his beaters. He showed his

pleasure in meeting George again, shook him firmly by
the hand and asked him about his progress. He went on to
invite him to call at the Hall before he returned to Brittwell Court.

As they walked home, George and Arthur tried to
figure out what motive there could be for this sudden
invitation. The Colonel hadn't specified a time but they
couldn't contain their curiosity for long, so the next
evening, at a time when he knew dinner would be over,
George presented himself at the front door. He was
ushered into Sir Albert's study and offered a drink. They
talked of fairly mundane things for a while, then George
was asked if he were happy in his present situation. He
told Sir Albert truthfully that, although he eventually
wanted to reach the top of his profession, for the moment
he was well satisfied. The Colonel came to the point. He
told him that a close associate, Squire Foljamb of Osberton Hall, was in need of a butler; he intimated that if
George should be interested the job was as good as his.
The neighbouring estate of Osberton was well known to
George; the Foljamb family were well respected in the
district and thought to be good employers; the position
of butler in their service was a very good one. George was
momentarily taken aback.

He thanked Sir Albert and said he would like a little
time to think it over. He wanted time to talk it over with
his parents and his brother, to consider what a change like
this could mean to him.

The position was higher than his present employment
as footman and another rung up the ladder was always of
interest to George. However, it was an entirely different
department of 'gentleman's service' and would mean
being in full charge of the domestic staff below stairs. He
was very young to take on such responsibility, for butlers
were generally older and more experienced men and their
orders were more readily obeyed than those given by a

younger man. There was much more to being a butler than just opening the front door to visitors and taking their hats and cloaks. He and the housekeeper would have full charge of the running of the household, from ordering the correct amount of provisions to keeping the domestic books straight, as well as settling any problems that might arise below stairs. Tempting as the offer might be, George had to be quite sure in his own mind that he could hold down such a position of trust.

His family were delighted, as he knew they would be. His mother was especially pleased, for it would mean that her son would be near home again. Arthur, too, had missed his companionship, and not unnaturally they were all proud that George had been offered such a position. After a good deal of thought, he decided to accept the position. As soon as he had told Sir Albert, an interview with Squire Foljamb was arranged, and within the next hour he was walking up the long drive to Osberton Hall.

It was certainly the most straightforward interview he had ever known. Squire Foljamb was a most genial man, who liked to cut all the red tape and, so long as the references were good, to judge the applicant's character himself. In this case he had clearly taken Sir Albert Whitaker's recommendation and offered George the job without more ado. His duties were outlined, the salary settled, and it was agreed that he should join the staff at the end of the month. The whole procedure hadn't taken more than half an hour.

On his return to Brittwell Court George tendered his resignation, explaining that the only reason for his departure was the prospect of a higher position. This was generally understood by both servant and master, a thing to be expected if a man was to reach the top of his profession. So, when the month was up, George started his new life with the Foljamb family. He did so with a certain amount of apprehension, but soon discovered he was able to settle well to his duties as butler. The other members of the staff were a cheerful lot, who knew their duties perfectly, and so there was no problem about their taking orders from the new young butler. The atmosphere was a happy one but, as in all big houses, there was the usual hierarchy among the servants. This meant that except for the housekeeper, there was no other servant on George's level, and he was expected to maintain a certain aloofness that didn't suit his character at all.

Squire Foljamb was a good master but a man of curious contradictions. He was justly proud of his widely-known wildlife sanctuary, and yet he rode to hounds at every possible opportunity and apparently spared no thought for the luckless fox, which almost invariably ended by being torn to shreds by a pack of fifty-two hounds. To George it was a nauseating sport, but servants were not supposed to hold opinions, let alone air them. The Squire owned a fine stable, and the family had been noted huntsmen from 1871, when Mr Frank Foljamb had assumed mastership of the Burton hounds. After each meet there were dinners and hunt balls for the entertainment of the Squire's influential friends and followers of the hunt. The main staircase of Osberton Hall was lined with animals' heads, macabre trophies of previous kills. On such occasions, while carrying out his duties and mingling with the guests, George would often overhear a lurid description of the way in which their latest quarry had met its end; whether it had turned to make a last brave stand against impossible odds, or whether the poor creature had screamed in terror until the fangs of the hounds had silenced it for ever. George would leave the room feeling sick and, if those gathered there could have read his thoughts, he wouldn't have remained as butler for long. It amazed him that these otherwise decent people could find such obvious joy in the suffering of any small creature.

It was pure accident that George upset the important Boxing Day meet. About forty riders of both sexes were assembled at the front of the Hall, all bubbling over with excitement. The first whip was doing his best to control fifty-two extremely hungry hounds. Huntsmen might hotly deny it, but the hounds were kept on very short rations for several days before a hunt so that they would be keener to seek out the quarry and make a satisfactory kill. The opposite was the case with the huntsmen themselves, who sat on horse-back while being served with hot refreshments before setting out. George, who led the procession of footmen outside, carried a huge butler tray laden with hot sausage rolls, thin toast spread with caviar, smoked salmon sandwiches, chicken pasties and stuffed olives. Immediately behind him, footmen carried the huge bowl of hot punch and large trays of crystal glasses. Hounds were milling around, sniffing at everything. As George approached the first rider, the lead dog got the scent of the piping hot tit-bits. That was all it needed to bring the whole pack, hurling themselves at him in hungry determination.

Taken completely by surprise, George found himself flat on his back and the entire contents of the tray scattered over the ground. As he fell back he collided with the footmen behind him and they too went flying in an undignified heap among the fragments of broken glass. Seconds later there was not a crumb left; the hounds had scoffed the lot, including the stuffed olives. The first whip's efforts to muster them were unavailing. After this the fox could have sauntered by, dragging his brush, without being spotted.

Needless to say, there was no kill on that occasion and, although everyone present was terribly disappointed, they sportingly put it down to sheer bad luck. They made up for it by having a riotous time at the hunt ball later that evening. George was not held in any way responsible for the unfortunate incident and most people showed great concern until they were sure he wasn't hurt. He even came in for a lot of good-natured teasing during the evening's frolics.

By this time he had been in the service of the Foljamb family for several months and he had become quite a favourite. They liked his pleasant manner and the efficient way in which he carried out his duties. So, apparently, did many of the friends who came to Osberton. Sometimes he would be present when one of the Squire's guests made a comment about him.

'You know, you really do have a treasure in Slingsby. He seems to know what is required almost before one knows it oneself, and that is very rare in butlers these days.'

George was fortunate in that he only ever heard praise of himself, but it would have been all the same if the remark had been to his discredit, for it was taken for granted that servants were discussed in their presence as though they were not there.

After almost a year as butler at Osberton George was well acquainted with most of the staff, both inside and out. One of the grooms in particular seemed to enjoy a chat whenever the opportunity arose. On one of his free afternoons, when George was walking round the estate, he stopped to chat with this new friend. During their conversation the groom was astounded to learn that George didn't ride, and suggested that he should give him lessons. At first George refused, but the groom was so insistent that against his better judgment, he gave in, and it was arranged that they should begin on his next full day off.

As the appointed day drew nearer, George wished that

he hadn't been so rash, but he was reluctant to back out and hoped it would rain. However, the morning was a fine one with just a nip in the air. Just the day for a canter, he was told when he reached the stables. He watched the groom lead the mare out, and was assured she was a docile creature. George had taken the precaution of bringing a few cubes of sugar, just to make sure the animal stayed that way. She took the sugar like a lamb, and even allowed him to fondle her muzzle.

'You're sure she's suitable for a beginner?' George asked for the umpteenth time.

'Ay' she's reet enough,' the groom replied with a grin. 'If she went any slower she'd stop altogether.'

The mare was already saddled and, feeling a little more assured, George decided to risk it. With difficulty he managed to climb into the saddle. To his relief the mare behaved perfectly. He took courage and, on the groom's instructions, they began to move off.

The groom had been right about one thing: the mare didn't seem to fancy the morning ride any more than George did. First she went backwards, then she went sideways, no doubt knowing that she had a novice on her back. Eventually, with more instructions, he managed to get her to go forward very slowly and, once he had got into the rhythm of the horse's movement, he began to enjoy the lovely scenery and the crisp morning air.

Then the groom's mount began to get frisky, pulling to get her head. It was obvious she loved a gallop and the pace was too slow for her. It suited George, however, and he was content to let the little mare take her time. All went well until they had to climb a steep bank to the bridle-path that skirted the estate. The groom's mount took it in one leap, but George's mare stood stock still and firmly refused to move. Both men tried everything to coax her to the top but their efforts were in vain. Even when the groom pulled hard on the rein, she laid her ears back and pulled in the opposite direction, and he began to get exasperated at this show of wilfulness.

'Give her your heel, George. Show her who's boss,' the groom advised.

George had an idea she already knew who was boss but tentatively did as he was told. When this also proved useless, the groom, who was not accustomed to being defied, leaned forward in the saddle and gave the mare a smart clip on the hind-quarters with his riding crop. What followed would have graced any rodeo arena, for the docile little mare suddenly turned into a lashing fury of flying hooves, with George hanging on for dear life. Swinging her hind-quarters back and forth as though she was dancing the rumba, she was determined to dislodge her rider. As she threw her hind legs into the air, George came a real cropper. She careered off in the direction of the stables, leaving George on the ground firmly convinced that every bone in his body must be broken. He spent the rest of that day soaking in a hot bath and rubbing himself with liniment. That was enough riding for him. In future he decided to stick to his favourite pastime of searching out the history and points of interest around the places where he worked.

Although George was happy at Osberton, he began to feel restless after about eighteen months. He had become competent in his duties as butler, but he was not really temperamentally suited to the job. As a footman he had become accustomed to a faster pace, the dressing for dinner, the bright, entertaining atmosphere and the companionship of his colleagues, and he missed all that. A butler's position was a lonely one. He had to maintain a rigid reserve and stand apart from the rest of the below-stairs staff. He had succeeded to a great extent in adopting the required butler attitude, but he was still too young to be expected to act like a stern father when two high-spirited kitchen maids were up to their larks and he was dying to laugh his head off. He had reached the top of the tree in this branch of service and he felt trapped in a humdrum existence, where the high-light of the day was serving afternoon tea in the drawing room. He missed the bright bustle of preparation for a big dinner party – and, yes, he even missed the crowded London streets, which was something he thought he would never do. If he was to leave how could he explain it to Sir Albert Whitaker, who had recommended him for the fine position in the first place? One didn't move from one position to another in gentleman's service without a valid reason. He could get himself branded as unreliable. Even his parents couldn't understand why he wasn't satisfied, so how could he expect Squire Foljamb to see his point of view? However, he decided to jump that hurdle when he got to it. On his next day off he went along to the same agency that had found him the position of footman to Brittwell Court and entered his name for a position as footman again.

It was nearly two months before a letter arrived informing him of a position of third footman to Welbeck Abbey, the home of the Duke and Duchess of Portland. Now was the time for explanations. He asked for a personal appointment with Squire Foljamb, feeling that it was only fair to show his gratitude for the very fair treament he had received at Osberton, and to try to explain why it was he wished to leave the Squire's service. He was relieved to discover that it was not so difficult after all. The Squire understood perfectly and wished him luck in his new position. This done, George prepared himself to join the staff of Welbeck Abbey at the end of the month.

❦ 8 ❧
Welbeck Abbey

W elbeck Abbey is still known as one of the largest and most beautiful estates in the midland and northern counties. When George arrived there the parkland stretched as far as the eye could see. A herd of deer grazed contentedly, and stately oaks and elms blended naturally into the background of Sherwood Forest. The fifty-two acres of pleasure gardens consisted of rose walks, herbaceous borders, natural lakes and broad sweeping lawns. The shrubberies were a cool delight, with a collection of plants from all over the world, while closer to the house the intricately designed flower beds resembled a lovely tapestry when viewed from the upper floors. There was a large outdoor skating rink, tennis courts and almost every other sporting amenity. The stables, about the size of a village, boasted a great number of the most famous thoroughbred horses in the country. A 'gallop', some 1,270 feet in length with a fully glazed roof, was a unique feature which ensured that the horses could be exercised in all weathers.

Dairy farms, which formed a large part of the vast estate, were equipped with the most up-to-date machinery of the time. Welbeck Abbey even had its own fire-fighting unit, complete with engine, reels of hose and all the other necessary requirements. The kitchen gardens were immense and there were acres of glasshouses which provided exotic flowers and fruit all year round. The orchid house could only be compared with those in the Royal Botanical Gardens. There were enormous vineries too.

George, who had marvelled at Rufford Abbey's size and beauty, was even more amazed by Welbeck, where there seemed to be as many rooms underground as there were above. The magnificent grand ballroom, which measured 159 feet by 63 feet, was a miracle of construction at the time it was built in 1875, for it had no supporting pillars. Mirrors lined the walls, giving the impression of infinity and from the painted ceiling hung four splendid chandeliers. Twenty-eight smaller ones were suspended from the hammer beams and sixty-four bracket lights with matching lustres adorned the walls.

Miles of subterranean passages led out in all directions from the house. But perhaps the most ingenious device was the underground railway, which had been installed to bring the food from the kitchens. It linked up with an intricate hydraulic lift system, which served all floors of the house and saved the legs of those who made up the huge staff.

The indoor staff alone were numbered in hundreds, for there was constant entertaining at Welbeck. King Edward VII often visited, and divided his time between Welbeck and Rufford during the racing seasons; this prospect pleased George for it brought closer his boy-hood ambition to meet the King face to face. At Rufford Abbey there had been a brief glimpse of His Majesty at a distance; now George would be serving at just such a beautiful banquet table as he had seen there earlier only through a crack in the doors.

George was given a few days to acquaint himself with his duties and to find his way about the mansion and grounds. The footmen's rooms, which he shared with his five colleagues, were on a much grander scale than those at Brittwell Court. His state livery was almost regal. The rich velvet cut-away coat, in a deep shade of wine, had the usual Byron collar and gold braid. With it went a shirt of fine Nottingham lace, with ruffled cravat and cuffs to match. White doeskin breeches, long white silk stock-ings, black shoes with silver buckles and a gold brocade waistcoat completed the ensemble. A silver wig replaced the old method of powdering the hair, and cut the dress-ing time down by half.

The day livery consisted of a black tail-coat, with a dog-tooth check waistcoat, both with monogrammed buttons, a starched shirt, with a high winged collar and a white bow tie. The only grouch George had was that the high, heavily-starched collar could turn into a saw which cut into his neck in the hot weather. The full-dress livery was worn on state occasions and in the evenings when dinner was served. During the day the footmen worked on a rota, so that there were always two on duty all the time. Their meals were taken in the servants' hall, where they were waited on by lower servants. They had their set days off and one long weekend in three, but apart from this they were on duty from six in the morning until the family retired for the night. Although the hours were long, there was always plenty of time when they did nothing at all, and no one minded if they had more than one break for refreshment. As long as they were on duty to answer the bell, they were never expected to work themselves to death.

The Duke and Duchess of Portland were good employers. Most of their staff had a job for life, were well cared for in the estate's own hospital block when they were ill, and at such times nothing was deducted from their wages. This, at a time when the working classes had no privileges, or indeed any help from the Government, was a real consideration. Many in service were certainly treated badly and, in some houses, were under-paid. George always referred to those who put up a fine front, conserving their wealth often at the expense of their staff, as the 'jumped-up rich'; such, however, was never the case in houses of any importance, like Welbeck, Rufford and Osberton. The real landed gentry and titled heads had no need to starve or ill-treat their servants, and often provided work where no other was available. Throughout his life George always held his employers in high regard. He was fortunate in that he never worked for the jumped-up rich people and always maintained that this was the difference between gentleman's service and domestic service.

The first time George set eyes on the Duchess Winifred he lost his heart to her. He was of an age when most young men have a definite idea of what the perfect woman should be, and the Duchess fitted that image for George in every detail. She was tall and willowy, with a regal deportment. Her delicate complexion reminded him of Dresden china and she possessed a smile that would charm a bird off a branch. He could well believe that no one had ever seen her in an ugly mood. She was full of fun and she was particularly fond of dancing. All the staff admired her, and Duke William adored her.

It was not long before his fellow footmen, a lively lot, were teasing George over what they called his crush on the Duchess. This he took all in good part, it was the sort of thing he had missed during his lonely post as butler. There was plenty of comradeship in the footmen's rooms where, as they cleaned their livery, they would relate amusing incidents that had occurred in the various places of their employ. After his visit to Ireland, George was able to contribute to the fun. Such confidences were never carried beyond their own quarters, of course, for personal servants had to be as discreet as the three wise monkeys who see all, hear all and say nothing.

Entertaining at Welbeck Abbey was on a grand scale. The Duchess was never happier than when she was planning a ball or a large dinner party. She especially loved to dress up, and many of her balls were attended in fancy dress and domino masks. She would be as excited as a child in her enthusiasm and her own costume would be a carefully guarded secret until she made her appearance on the night of the ball. These big functions meant extra work for the staff, but somehow the gaiety of the occasion was infectious and nearly everyone took part in making the evening a success. Afterwards the Duchess always posted a personal note of appreciation on the baize notice board for all the staff to read, and they would glow with pride at her Grace's praise.

As the racing season approached preparations began for the King's visit. The Doncaster race course wouldn't have been the same without his portly figure in the royal stand. A fever of excitement ran through the Abbey as the frantic cleaning and polishing went on in all departments. On the day of His Majesty's arrival the red carpet was rolled down the front steps. George and his fellow footmen, in their freshly cleaned liveries, took their places at the top of the steps and spaced around the grand entrance hall. Then the cavalcade of carriages, led by the King's personal carriage, was seen approaching up the stately drive. As the formal greeting took place George noticed with amusement how the King's little dog Caesar obeyed the call of nature against one of the stone pedestals and how his owner paused, lead in hand, to await his pet's pleasure.

The King generally rested in his private rooms immediately after his journey, so things would be quiet for a while, until the evening's entertainment got under way. The menu had been planned long beforehand and the important things had already been done. The banquet table had been dressed, and the great underground ballroom floor had been waxed to a high polish. Until the dinner gong sounded, the personal servants had little to do. During this time the footmen donned large wraparound aprons to protect their state liveries, which had to be immaculate when they attended at table.

For the rest of the afternoon George and his colleagues killed time in the servants' hall, for officially they were still on duty if the bell in their department rang. The gorgeous aromas of the food began to filter through from the vast kitchens and the general activity mounted to fever pitch as the time drew near. Then it was off with the aprons as the footmen made a final inspection of the dining room before the banquet began. They checked that the place settings were correct, that the cruets were in position and that the flowers were still as fresh as when they were cut. When they were satisfied that everything was in perfect order, they took up their places like sentinels with their backs to the walls of the corridor along which the guests would come in pairs to the dining room.

The King always led this splendid procession, escorting the Duchess of Portland. They would be followed by the Duke escorting Queen Alexandra, and so on in order of title or rank. Chattering and laughing in their silks and brocades, the guests passed through the magnificent doors to their places at the dinner table. Then the footmen's work really began. The hum of the hydraulic lift told them that the first course was on its way up. As speedily as possible, but without seeming to hurry, it had to be served piping hot. Then each footman, according to his own position, would stand straight-backed and watchful to see that a cruet had not been moved out of reach. It was part of their job to anticipate the needs of every guest before they had to ask.

One state dinner provided an incident which George found particularly funny to recall. It occurred during the main course, when the footmen were using the newest method of serving vegetables. The containers were circular, about the size of a small cartwheel, and were divided into sections, each of which held a different vegetable. A heated element in the base ensured the food would remain hot and the footman held a heat-proof handle at the back with one hand, leaving a free hand to remove the lid. In this way the guests were able to help themselves to as little or as much as they required. It was much quicker than juggling with large tureens.

The first and second footmen were serving the top table and, as etiquette demanded, the ladies were served first. The two ladies placed on either side of His Majesty were so busy competing for his attentions that neither was putting her mind to the food being offered. Fashions had begun to alter in this new Edwardian era, and certain dinner gowns were now cut rather lower in the neckline. In fact some were so daring that the footmen had been instructed to avert their eyes when serving a lady at the dinner table. So what with the lady's attention being on other things and the footman averting his eyes, it was fairly certain that a catastrophe would occur. The second footman held the dish and the lady in question began to help herself while she continued to give the King all her attention. In so doing she put too much pressure on the container and the footman felt the handle begin to slip.

Automatically he tightened his grip as the dish began to spin; the jolt was enough to dislodge a very small but very hot potato, which shot straight down the front of the lady's gown. The lady began to shriek with pain, thus drawing the attention of everyone at the table. Without stopping to think of the consequences, the footman plunged a hand into her cleavage and removed the hot potato.

In the ensuing silence, George could hear himself breathe. There was a mixture of horror and disbelief on all the faces there, while the scarlet-faced footman waited for the axe to fall. He had probably saved the lady from a very nasty burn, nevertheless he had taken an unforgivable liberty. Then the King began to laugh and this broke the tension. And because the King laughed, the lady also began to laugh, and within the next few minutes the dining room was in an uproar. King Edward slapped his thigh and rocked in his chair with mirth. His amusement certainly saved the day for one very embarrassed footman. Afterwards, in the privacy of the footmen's rooms, his colleagues ribbed him unmercifully, saying that they would never have thought he was that kind of chap.

As the fifth of November approached plans were made for the traditional Welbeck Abbey bonfire party. The Duchess had arranged to have a gigantic firework display, a huge bonfire and all kinds of games in the grounds. A thick tarpaulin sheet was spread over a large area in case it should rain and dinner was to be served in what we now know as barbecue style. The Duchess was going about in a froth of excitement that carried the staff along with her enthusiasm.

On the evening of the fifth the guests began to arrive, all warmly wrapped for the occasion. The gentlemen wore thick overcoats with astrakhan collars and hats to match, and the ladies came in their sables and ermine. The evening began with drinks served in the library, and after the right spirit had been reached, the party went down towards the lake where the huge bonfire was burning, fanned by a light breeze. Fortunately the weather had remained dry. Someone remarked that it wouldn't dare have rained when the Duchess Winifred had planned such a party. Nevertheless, a large marquee had been erected in case the weather took a nasty turn. George and his fellow footmen were posted behind long trestle tables to serve hot punch to sharpen the guests' appetite for venison steaks later on. These were cooked on gridirons and the chef was already basting and turning them to perfection.

Then came the great moment for the firework display, and what fireworks they were, to be sure! Never before had such splendid things been seen in the neighbouring country villages. Coloured feathers trailed across the sky and catherine wheels seemed to spin endlessly. A bonfire the size of a haystack was surmounted by the traditional guy, which had been put together laboriously by the gardeners. The flames shot up to a great height, but nobody seemed to mind going home smelling like smoked kippers. After the party was over, the footmen found that it was a devil of a job to restore their livery to its usual immaculate condition. The white doeskin breeches were covered in black smuts and the silver wigs had turned a dark grey. George and his colleagues hoped that the Duchess would forgo any further bonfire parties.

Christmas was a splendid occasion and George was not too disappointed that he was unable to go home. He rather wanted to be part of the celebrations he had heard so much about. Indeed, many of the staff who had very little to go home to anyway actually preferred to stay.

New Year's Eve at Welbeck was the favourite celebration of the year, eagerly anticipated by all, from the Duchess down to the lowest kitchen maid. As at Rufford

Abbey, it was one time when protocol was to some extent relaxed. The staff were allowed to arrange their own ball in the servants' hall, and just for once a kitchen maid could associate with a footman and a parlour maid with the butler. Duties would be carried out in the normal way, but after dinner was over and the guests and family had withdrawn to the ballroom, the servants would begin to enjoy their own dancing. They were still on call, but only when it was really necessary. So long as a footman remained sober to serve the champagne for the midnight toast to the New Year, they could celebrate until the early hours of the next day, if they so wished. Sometime during the evening it was traditional for the Duke and Duchess to leave their own party to make an appearance below stairs to wish all their staff a happy new year.

There were the usual lavish preparations for New Year's Eve, which was to culminate in a grand fancy dress ball. There was speculation among the staff about the costume Her Grace was likely to wear. A casual hint from above stairs suggested she might choose to be Prince Charming, but this could easily be a 'red herring' put out by the Duchess herself. The secret was always well kept.

While the family were away before Christmas, the footmen took the opportunity to make sure their liveries were immaculate in readiness for the New Year's grand ball. In the footmen's room, all six men would be busy with cleaning fluids and metal polish. They chatted together as they removed spots and polished buttons. The first footman, who had been longest in the service of Welbeck Abbey, was describing some of the costumes he had seen on previous occasions. He related how comical it was to see an eminent gentleman, dressed as a monkey, trying to cope with his tail while he danced the Lancers. It was trodden on so often by the other dancers, that in the

end he lost it altogether, which automatically turned the
gentleman into a baboon. All he needed, said the footman, was a blue posterior, to make him a prime specimen
for the London Zoo.

Then as usual when men get together, the subject
turned to the fair sex and they began, not disrespectfully,
to discuss and compare the charms of the many society
beauties of that time. One of the older footmen said that
Miss Lillie Langtry, who had been such a success on the
London stage in his youth, was his idea of a real beauty.
Another sang the praises of certain other ladies whose
charms were renowned and remarked that he wouldn't
mind taking any of them out for the evening, given the
chance. A third footman, looking up from his chores
with a grin, said he didn't think they would appreciate a
pint at the local instead of champagne. Nor could he
imagine them eating fish and chips from a newspaper.

They turned to George, who so far had kept out of the
conversation, and asked him who would be his choice.
Without hesitation, he told them that in his opinion none
of these ladies could hold a candle to their own Duchess
for beauty, charm and sweet disposition. His praise of
Her Grace was so fulsome that it brought on a barrage of
leg-pulling from the other men.

'For heaven's sake, don't ever let the Duke hear you
going off about his missus like that, or you may end up
on a dish with an apple in your mouth.'

George laughed at their teasing, and maintained he
would give half his week's pay to be able to dance with
her. He was a good dancer himself and he had often
admired the Duchess's skill and grace on the dance floor.
His remark almost started a riot among the other footmen. One thing led to another, until one said that if
George was serious about his ambition there was only
one way it could be achieved without detection – providing he had the pluck to do it. George listened, horrified, as

his colleague outlined his plan. He had to get himself a costume and a domino mask and, when the ball was in full swing, mingle with the guests while the others covered up for him. After he had achieved his dance with the Duchess, he could bolt up the back stairs, change back into his livery and still be in time to serve the champagne on the stroke of twelve.

It had all started as a joke and George tried to laugh it off, but he wasn't going to be allowed to back out. They laid a wager of half a sovereign from each of them that he dare not go through with this hare-brained scheme. It was now a matter of honour and George felt forced to accept the wager.

❦ 9 ❦
The Duchess and the Wager

Before he could change his mind, George's challengers set about the details of their plan, arranging on the next half day's leave for George and another footman to visit a small costumier in Worksop. Once the situation seemed irreversible, George began to fancy himself in something dashing, but found that most of the romantic costumes had already been hired out. However, there was a cavalier costume with a handsome plumed hat that caught his eye.

'I'll try that one,' he said.

The assistant looked doubtful. 'I don't think it will be large enough, sir.'

George carried it into the fitting room to make sure. Unfortunately the assistant was right; the only thing that fitted was the plumed hat. He couldn't button the embroidered waistcoat and the trousers were decidedly tight. All the other costumes were so ordinary that he felt he would stick out like a sore thumb if he wore any of them in such a grand assembly. He hoped the situation would end this risky game, but suddenly the helpful assistant produced another costume.

'Try this one, sir. It seems appropriate.'

It was the red and white striped suit of a court jester, complete with cap and bells and a pair of slippers with the toes turned up. George had no alternative but to try it on, and, having done so, had to admit that not only was it a perfect fit, but that he looked rather well in it too. He put on the black domino mask and came out to be inspected, the silver bells tinkling as he moved. The other footman began to laugh.

'Blimey, George; if the Duchess doesn't see you, she will certainly hear you coming. If you want to surprise her, mate, I should take the clappers out of those blooming bells.'

The die was cast and there was no turning back. On the way home George had grave qualms about the venture. He wondered however he could have been persuaded into this foolhardy situation.

By the time New Year's Eve arrived, George was in a blue funk. Had there not been so much to do, he might have been inclined to bolt for it.

Dinner was to be served at eight o'clock, and would take approximately an hour and a half. Then the ladies would adjourn to change into their costumes, while the gentlemen did likewise and enjoyed brandy and cigars. As soon as the dining room was vacated the maids would begin to clear as quickly as possible, supervised by the footmen who had to see that the best silver and china were returned safely to the housekeeper. They could then relax until they served supper at half past ten. Between then and midnight, George would have his chance to win his wager.

As darkness fell the lights from every window in Welbeck Abbey streamed out to warm the chilly evening and masses of tiny coloured lights had been entwined into the trees outside. Carriages had been arriving since early in the day. As each party of guests arrived they were shown to their suites to rest and prepare for the festivities to come. The servants had started their celebrations early in the afternoon, knowing that later on there would be time to draw breath. They had taken a drop of 'Dutch courage' in between chopping, mixing and stirring, then chewed parsley to keep the breath sweet. All day the most appetising smells drifted round the kitchens.

In the dining room a huge floral arch spanned the banquet table. It was cleverly composed of fruit, flowers and ferns, and a large silver bell hung from the centre. The spotless table linen, with the table napkins folded into the design of a cock's comb, and the sparkle of silver and crystal, never failed to enchant George.

About a hundred guests sat down to a dinner that would be beyond most people's imagination, and champagne flowed like water. The climax came when the Duchess produced her New Year's surprise, a huge box of what must have been the most expensive bonbons ever made. As the guests pulled these elaborate crackers, there were gasps of astonishment when pieces of costly jewellery fell out on to the table. There were exquisite little gold fob watches, garnet rings, gold brooches and pearls for the ladies, and diamond tie-pins and gold cigar piercers for the gentlemen. The Duke and Duchess sat amused while the ladies sorted and exchanged with one another, until each had the piece of her choice.

During the time the above-stairs staff had been busy with their duties at the banquet, those below stairs had filled in their time by laying long trestle tables in readi-

ness for their own special meal. Although it may not have
been presented in quite the same way, there was certainly
no shortage of food. There was a huge ham, a whole
Stilton cheese and a sucking pig that had been roasted to
perfection. There was plenty of beer, wine and even a
magnum of champagne with which to toast the New
Year. All this was a welcome sight to the footmen, who
had watched others tucking in for the last hour. George's
enthusiasm for food might have been keener on this
occasion if he hadn't his dance with the Duchess on his
mind. If luck wasn't with him, he might find himself
without anything for which to celebrate the New Year.

Strains of dance music were now filtering through the
house and guests were appearing in a great variety of
costumes, some of them most ingenious. Then at last the
Duchess made her entrance dressed as Nell Gwynne. The
tightly laced bodice of the London orange-seller suited
her to perfection. Her hair, dressed in ringlets, was
topped by a lacy mob-cap, and she carried a small basket
of oranges. Her black lace domino mask was supposed to
hide her identity, but there was no mistaking the poise
and mannerisms that everyone knew so well. She was
outstanding in every way and it would have taken more
than a slender mask to disguise that. As George stood at
his post just inside one of the great doors of the ballroom,
he absorbed the beauty of the scene, the unbelievable
glitter of those magnificent chandeliers, the reflections in
the mirrors of an endless whirl of dancers in their gaily-
coloured costumes, and the sweet smell of the ladies'
perfumes.

The time to serve supper approached. At ten thirty the
footmen began their stately walk into the ballroom. They
carried butler trays laden with delicious tit-bits which
were works of art in themselves. The chef had spent
hours on these ambrosial morsels for this special occasion. More champagne was opened, the lights were

dimmed to a romantic glow, and they would remain so
until the stroke of midnight. Then they would blaze
again and hundreds of coloured balloons would be
released from nets attached to the ceiling, while the New
Year was toasted in enthusiastically.

When supper had been served, the footmen arranged
between themselves a shuttle service from the ballroom
to the servants' hall and back. In this way they were
always available if needed, but they were also able to take
turns to enjoy the fun below stairs. This was the time for
George to win his wager, and his colleagues began to give
him meaningful signals.

'Come on then, get on with it.'

So, quaking a little, George made his way up the back
stairs to the footmen's rooms, where he quickly donned
his jester's suit. Peering at himself in the mirror, he felt
fairly satisfied that no one would easily recognise him,
though he was a little worried about his slight accent.
Having once gained Her Grace's company on the dance
floor, he could only hope that she didn't wish to converse
while they danced. However, there was no time to dwell
on the situation. As he entered the ballroom he was
relieved to find that, apart from the odd glance here and
there, he seemed to be accepted as just another guest in
fancy dress. He moved forward as casually as he could to
where the Duchess was standing with a group of other
people who seemed not to notice they had been joined by
a court jester. The musicians began to play a Veleta.
George noticed Her Grace beginning to tap her foot in
time to the music. This was his chance. Before his nerve
deserted him he stepped up to her, bowed low and said
the words he had been practising for weeks.

'May I have the pleasure, madam?'

The Duchess smiled and led the way out on to the
dance floor. Their steps fitted perfectly as they mingled
with the other dancers; George's fear of detection began

to fade as the sheer pleasure of the dance took over. No one showed the least concern as the pert footman swirled his Duchess in their midst.

The Veleta came to an end, and George was about to lead her back to her company when the music began again with a military two-step. It was George's favourite dance and much to his delight the Duchess seemed to take it for granted that they should continue. It was gratifying to realise that she was so obviously enjoying the dance too. Not a single step went wrong and not once did he crush her feet. Just as the dance was nearing its end, the Duchess broke the silence.

'You are an excellent dancer, young man,' she said.

George thanked her, and murmured something to the effect that, with such an accomplished partner, how could he fail?

She gave a musical laugh and replied: 'Very well said, but if I didn't know you were my third footman, I would declare you were a professional.'

George felt prickles growing at the back of his neck and wished that the floor would open and swallow him up. They continued the dance with George frantically searching his mind for an excuse for this frivolous behaviour. Then, as the dance finished, she chuckled again.

'Don't look miserable,' she whispered. 'It's New Year's Eve, and I won't give you away.'

George led her back to her guests, bowed again and left as if the Devil was about to grab him. Outside the ballroom the footman at the top of the stairs patted him on the back.

'Come on, mate, get a move on, it's ten minutes to midnight.'

He dashed up the back stairs, where he quickly changed back into his livery. After a final look in the mirror to see that his wig was on straight, he went back to his post, thanking his luck that he wasn't packing his bags. He was back in good time to help with opening the champagne and on the stroke of twelve they carried in their laden trays again. The coloured balloons floated down and as the high-spirited revellers tussled with one another to gain possession of them, the footmen had to be very careful to keep out of the way. A huge quantity of champagne was cleared in seconds as everyone toasted the New Year. George offered his tray to the Duchess, who took one of the glasses with a sweet smile and what he thought to be a hint of mischief in her eyes. She was as good as her word: there was no reprimand and the incident was never referred to again.

Most of George's free days were spent in the company of his brother, who was still employed in the vineries of Rufford Abbey. The estates were very close and they both knew all the short cuts to reach one another quickly. On one such occasion Arthur told George of a rumour at Rufford that Lord Savile would soon be looking for a new footman, the first in rank to seven. George was interested, for although he was happy in his service to Welbeck Abbey, another step up the ladder was always a consideration. Arthur promised he would let him know when the post was definitely in the offing and a month later the position indeed became vacant.

'Get t'that agency, George, and be sharp about it,' Arthur advised. 'It'll not be vacant for long.'

By this time interviews held no fear for George, but there was a small problem. He had started his service life to Rufford Abbey as a lower-grade servant and knew he could be turned down for this very reason. Nevertheless, he was determined to try his luck, and hoped that his break in service to Rufford would at least give him a sporting chance.

The interview took place a week later and there were

ten other applicants. When he was called in, George found Lord Savile sitting at a desk scrutinising his credentials. He motioned George to sit down and spent the next few minutes pondering over the papers, leaving George to listen to the slow tick of a huge bracket clock on the wall. After what seemed an eternity, he looked up.

'I see that you have been in my service before.'

It was a statement rather than a question but anyway George had already decided to make a clean breast of the fact.

'That is so, sir.'

Lord Savile smiled and continued, 'I see that I gave you an excellent reference too.'

George waited.

'You seem to have made very good progress in your profession. I find this most satisfactory. But you do know of course that it is not the usual practice to promote a lower-grade servant to above stairs in the same house?'

George nodded. 'I do, sir, but I rather hoped that my long break from your service might make a difference to that rule.'

'Did you, indeed?' Lord Savile smiled again.

Then he went back to considering the papers in front of him, while George waited again in silence. At last he seemed to make his decision and looked again at George.

'I have decided to go against my better judgment on this occasion because you are obviously the best applicant for the post. You have the advantage of already knowing the routine of my house and this of course saves time, but I shall require your word that the Abbey rules shall be kept in all aspects, and that you will maintain the necessary protocol towards those you may have known under different circumstances. Do I make myself clear?'

George assured Lord Savile that this would be so, and after he had been given the details of the position, he left the agency feeling elated.

He tendered his resignation as soon as he returned to Welbeck and then went in search of his brother to impart the news. Arthur was taking his lunch in the little pub with a few of the other gardeners and, as George greeted them, another pint was called for. He was congratulated by all and Arthur was delighted that they would be in closer contact, but talking to these men he had known as a garden boy, George realised how difficult it was going to be to keep the promise he had made to Lord Savile. As soon as he was installed in his new post he knew that too much familiarity would be frowned upon and during working hours this would include his own brother. Their present gathering would have to be a sort of last fling; they all knew this, but tankards were filled repeatedly in acknowledgment that friendships didn't die simply because they all wore different uniforms.

❧ 10 ❧

Encounter with the King

George joined the staff of Rufford Abbey, for the second time, and spent the first few days familiarising himself with his new duties. He was relieved to find that those who had known him previously below stairs automatically accepted him in his risen status. Even the young maid who had given him his first glimpse of the inside of Rufford gave him the respect due to rank without the slightest sign of breaking protocol.

There were seven footmen to serve Rufford Abbey and the routine was virtually the same here as at Welbeck, with the exception that George was now senior in charge of his six colleagues and therefore had more responsibility. He had to acquaint himself with eighteen suites of rooms, all the state apartments, long galleries and corridors that went in all directions. When the bell rang to summon the footmen, he had to know exactly where to go and the quickest way to get there. Now he went from room to room, marvelling at the beauty and grandeur of it all. The King Edward VII suite was of special interest to him, with its pearl-inlaid furniture and huge bed canopied in yellow silk. Even the commode was a thing of great beauty. There was the George IV suite, the Halifax suite, the Lumley suite, the Ambassador's suite, Lord Elland's suite, the Stuart room, the Gable room, and the Venetian room; all of equal magnificence, through which George browsed with sheer delight. Rufford was a treasure-house of priceless paintings, antiques and many other works of art. George particularly loved the clock in the library, depicting Father Time, an old man carrying a scythe over his shoulder, and the huge tinted mirror at the top of the grand staircase. But he still disliked the cruel painting of 'The Boar Hunt' by Snyders. It had horrified him as a boy, and it still made him turn his head whenever he passed it.

George was well versed in his duties by the time his bespoke state livery arrived a month later, for the King's visit. Arthur did not see him in his livery until the day before the royal arrival. He came with the other garden-ers to decorate the Abbey, just as George had done, with the usual immense quantity of flowers, fruit and ferns. The footmen were on duty at certain positions about the house, and George stood at the great doors of the banquet room when Arthur entered with his loaded baskets. The instant he caught sight of George, it was as much as they both could do to keep their reserve. They could only acknowledge one another by sly winks, but George knew exactly what Arthur was thinking. The next time they were home together, Arthur told their parents, 'You should just see our George in his monkey suit. He looks a proper dandy.'

The King and his party duly arrived in the usual grand

manner and this time George stood proudly at the front entrance with his colleagues, in charge of the red carpet. His boyhood dream of serving His Majesty at top table was about to come true.

What he couldn't know until later, however, was that on this occasion he would make the biggest blunder of his career.

The same delectable menu had been carefully prepared for the occasion and the same mad whirl went on below stairs to see that everything went according to plan. As the first dinner gong sounded to bring the guests to the table, George took up his position with the other footmen along the crimson corridor to the dining room. The procession began with His Majesty escorting Lady Savile and so on in order of rank. The food began to arrive and George led the stately walk carrying the first course, a large tureen of turtle soup.

Everything went like clockwork, until the main course. The footmen stood back from the table keeping a sharp eye out for any irregularities. George suddenly noticed that one of the guests was in need of a cruet which had been moved too far down the table. He immediately took a handsome silver cruet from the sideboard and placed it in front of the gentleman who liberally peppered his spinach. At that same moment, George saw another footman making frantic signs to remove the cruet at once. He did so mystified. When clearing for the next course, his colleague explained, with a grin, why this particular cruet was so offensive. It was a casket containing the ashes of an ancestor to the Savile family.

King Edward stayed at Rufford for two weeks and it was during this time that George realised his second boyhood ambition, to speak with the King personally. He was taking his lunch and a tankard of beer, sitting in his shirt sleeves, when His Majesty appeared, unannounced, with his little dog at his heels. The kitchen

staff immediately stood to attention and George made a
grab for his jacket, but the King held up his hand.

'Please, do not let me disturb you. I am the intruder.'
He walked over to George and cast a covetous eye on the
tankard of beer.

'That looks exceedingly good. Do you think I might
join you?' he said.

George called for a glass, but the King waved it away.

'A tankard will do nicely, I think pewter improves the
flavour, don't you?'

George agreed, and drew off a foaming pint of the
draught beer and handed it to His Majesty, who took a
seat on the opposite side of the table, while his little dog
jumped up and sat beside George. The dog clearly had
ideas about the bread and cheese on George's plate, and
kept lifting one paw expectantly. This rather put George
on the spot, until the King saw the situation and laughed.

'I'm afraid my dog has no manners at all,' he said. 'He
will give you no peace until he gets some of your lunch.'

If the dog had belonged to anyone else, George would
have fed him tit-bits automatically. Now, with the
King's consent, he let Caesar finish what was left on the
plate.

The King explained that he was interested in the history of this particular part of the Abbey and asked George
numerous questions, which fortunately he was able to
answer. Then, having finished his beer, King Edward
thanked him and left as unpretentiously as he had arrived.

It was two more years before George began to get what
his brother called 'itchy feet' again. This time he wanted
the post of valet, the last step to reach his goal. He was
now twenty-three and had decided it was time to move
on. Once again he entered his name on the agency's lists
hopefully. Such top positions did not fall vacant very
often. It was several months before the familiar brown

envelope arrived, this time informing him of a post as valet to a certain Sir Frederick Orr Lewis. It contained the card of introduction and the time and date of the interview, which was to be held at the Regina Bureau in London. He applied for time off and caught the train to London.

The interview was at three o'clock in the afternoon and George took his place with eighteen other applicants and prepared for a long wait. The time spent twiddling one's hat in complete silence was always the most tedious part of these interviews; the alphabetical system always made George among the last to be called, so patience had to be a virtue. Two hours later he was introduced to the gentleman sitting behind the desk.

Sir Frederick Orr Lewis was in his late forties and, as a Canadian, he had a very different attitude towards conducting an interview from the stiff protocol observed by the English aristocracy on such occasions. The handshake on introduction was unusual and he didn't beat about the bush. He left George in no doubt what he would expect from his new valet and then went on to quote the benefits and salary before even looking at George's references. However, when he eventually turned his attention to George's credentials, he was as thorough as any other employer. After a few minutes, he sat back and looked at George again. He asked a few questions, some quite personal ones, which George answered without difficulty, and then the interview was over and George went back to his seat in the lobby. There was just one other applicant to go in, and another quarter of an hour ticked by. Then, to George's great satisfaction, he was called back and offered the job.

On his way home he had a lot to occupy his mind. A valet's work was very varied and there was no near colleague to consult or from whom to learn. Sir Frederick had said they would be travelling almost constantly, back and forth to Canada and the United States, and George wondered how his mother would react to this situation.

On his return to Rufford, George tendered his resignation. Later, over a pint of beer, Arthur took the news with mixed feelings. He gasped with surprise to hear the salary George would be receiving in his new position.

'By gum! I reckon he wants you to do murder for that sort of money.'

George had a week's holiday due to him and decided to spend it with his parents before starting in his new position. Arthur managed to get the weekend free, so they travelled home together. George's mother took the news calmly, but her expression showed apprehension at the mention of sea travel. It was obvious that she still harboured a fear of water, but she made no comment and the week was spent happily, until it was time to return and pack up.

They were bedding out for spring in the gardens at Rufford and everything looked orderly and peaceful. Saying goodbye to old friends was a poignant experience and, as he walked down the long drive, George already nursed a feeling of nostalgia.

~ II ~
Gentleman's Gentleman

G eorge hoped the glorious spring sunshine would be a good omen as he hailed a motor-cab outside King's Cross station. He helped the cabby to load his trunk on to the running board and stated his destination. Then they joined the congested London streets en route to the next episode in George's career.

The smart house in Lancaster Gate was far removed from the mansion he had left, but was nevertheless imposing in its own way. George rang the bell on the front door, which was opened by the butler, and stated his business. The butler snapped his fingers to bring a footman to cope with his luggage. George went to give him a hand with the heavy trunk, but the butler reproved him.

'That's not your job, sir. Will you please come this way?'

George followed him in, feeling the butler's attitude to be a little unnecessary.

'I don't mind giving a hand now and then, you know,' George told him.

'Maybe not, sir, but your duties will be to the master only. I'm sure Sir Frederick would think it most irregular.'

The butler informed George that Sir Frederick would not be at home until six o'clock that evening, and that he would ring for him on his return. In the meantime, he was to spend the day settling in.

As they went up the staircase, George was astonished at the grandeur and size of the house. From the outside, it gave no indication of such proportions. His own private rooms were the biggest surprise of all. He was to have his own bathroom, and there was everything he could possibly need, even writing-paper. When a maid appeared to do his unpacking, he thought the time had come to put his foot down. There were a few things he intended to do for himself, whatever the butler said.

Left alone, he did a bit of exploring. Sir Frederick's rooms were just across the corridor from his own. He found the study, where he had been told Sir Frederick would meet him later in the day and made a few mental notes about the house in general before going back to finish his unpacking. He met a maid coming out of his room who informed him she had run a bath for him. Apparently the butler had ordered this too, in case George wanted to freshen up after his journey. This time George accepted the courtesy without comment. As he wallowed in the warm suds, he had to admit this V.I.P. treatment rather agreed with him.

After his bath, George wrote a letter home on the smart headed paper and then rested on his bed for a while. At four o'clock the maid appeared with a tray of afternoon tea, for which he was very grateful. Then at six o'clock sharp, the bell summoned him to the study, where he found Sir Frederick sitting in a deep leather armchair, sipping a whisky and soda. He greeted George cheerfully and indicated the chair opposite for George to be seated. George sat, listening carefully to the long list of duties that would be expected of him. Apart from his holidays, which would be taken twice a year, and his day off, it seemed he would be on call from the time he ran his master's bath in the morning until the family retired for the night. He knew he could cope with most of the duties Sir Frederick mentioned without trouble, but was a little apprehensive on hearing that he would be in full charge of all the arrangements whenever they made an Atlantic crossing. George decided to jump that hurdle when he got to it. Sir Frederick then began to talk about the family, a sort of introduction beforehand. There were two daughters, aged eight and ten years, and a son in his teens who was away at Eton College. At the mention of 'Duncan', Sir Frederick smiled ruefully.

'I feel I should give you a warning about my son. He is rather high-spirited and as you are new to the household, I fear you may be rather vulnerable to his curious sense of humour. He can be exasperating, but don't take too much of his nonsense, George.'

It astounded George that Sir Frederick should find it necessary to give such a warning about his own son and he hoped that Duncan wasn't going to be the fly in the ointment. He was also surprised to hear Sir Frederick call him by his Christian name. He had no objections, of course, but it was unusual after the formality of English service. Then Sir Frederick suggested that he made himself known to the other members of the staff and George took his leave.

He knew from previous experience that it was always an advantage to be on good terms with cook and the housekeeper, so his first call was the kitchens. He found the staff marking time until they prepared dinner, which was served at eight o'clock in the evening. The kitchens were a far remove from those at Rufford Abbey, but they were well equipped and the dozen or so staff were equally well trained. At first, George was received with guarded reserve, but over a pot of tea he was able to break down their reserve with genial conversation. When he left, he felt that good will had been made.

The following morning he was up at six, bathed and dressed carefully to meet the first day in his new position. Cook had said that Sir Frederick's breakfast tray would be ready each morning and it was taken to him at seven thirty. Sir Frederick seems to have been less than a robust man: he was not chronically sick but suffered from stomach ulcers, insomnia and was generally delicate. So, bearing his master's breakfast tray, George entered the bedroom, drew back the curtains, set the tray across the bed and helped Sir Frederick to sit up amongst his pillows. He was relieved to find Sir Frederick sweet-tempered first thing in the morning and they exchanged pleasantries as though George had been there years instead of only hours. He asked George to lay out a suitable attire for town and while he enjoyed his braised kidneys and mushrooms, George chose a grey pin-striped suit, a cream silk shirt and a conservative tie. Then he went to run Sir Frederick's bath.

To dress one's gentleman meant exactly what it implied. The valet did practically everything, except wear the clothes himself. He helped his master into the bath and held the towel to wrap him when he got out. He held the trousers, so that all the gentleman had to do was to slip his legs into them. He tied his tie, adjusted braces, buttons and fastenings, put on his socks and laced his shoes. He brushed his hair, selected his tie-pin and tucked a handkerchief into his top pocket to finish the job. A good valet gave advice on the choice of his clothes, so good taste was essential, but George soon discovered that most of these many and varied duties relied more than anything on common sense.

Over the next few weeks George fitted in favourably with everyone. Lady Orr Lewis was charming and took a liking to George from their first meeting. It was fashionable then for a lady to have an escort to help her in and out of the car, open shop doors for her, carry purchases and tuck the rug round her knees in the cold weather. Lady Orr Lewis began to borrow George for this purpose whenever Sir Frederick was not in need of his services. He consulted George on his feelings about these extra duties to Her Ladyship, but George was quite content.

The two young daughters, Miss Ellen and Miss Jane, were nice children, and they also laid claim to George's attentions. When time permitted, he would play ball with them and indulge them in all kinds of games that little girls like to play. He got on well with the staff, the two pet Pekingese dogs and even the parrot, who had been brought home by a sea-faring uncle to the family. 'Polly' was an accomplished mimic and could copy the human voice exactly. It often caused offence to sensitive people who came to the house and on these occasions he would be banished to the harness room, where his already wide vocabulary gained another facet. It was the first time George had heard a parrot swear with a public school accent. It was amusing to hear Her Ladyship complain.

'I really can't imagine where Polly hears such terrible language.'

Being in service to this colonial family was greatly different from the life-style of the English aristocracy. Rules were more relaxed and Sir Frederick maintained that a well paid and happy staff gave their loyalty and best service automatically. George had to admit that, in this case at any rate, it paid off. Protocol was observed and there was still the division of above- and below-stairs servants, but they themselves seemed to prefer this, so it was seldom anyone stepped out of place. Foster, the butler, was not such a stuffed shirt that first impressions had given, and George found a friend in Marshall, the chauffeur.

The London season was approaching, the grand event of the year. During this time, the rich and notable would flock to take up residence in their smart town houses and all the window boxes would suddenly burst into bloom. Most would bring their own gardeners to plant them out and there was great competition in these floral displays. Gaily striped awnings were erected over windows and front doors and the ladies of quality would take the air in pretty summer dresses, carrying dainty silk and lacy parasols. The royal parks were a grand sight, with the smart carriages and fine high-stepping horses. The gentlemen raised their hats to the ladies who exercised their little lap-dogs, or who rode with dignity in Rotten Row.

It was an important time for those with eligible daughters and no effort was spared to see that, in 'coming out', she met only the right kind of people. Mothers were busy thumbing their way through *Burke's Peerage* and *Who's Who* to find suitable young bachelors as possible escorts for daughters who had to be launched into society with a flourish of expensive entertainments, new clothes, hair styles and the all important gown in which they would be presented at Court. It was a profitable time for the charm schools, beauty parlours and top dress designers and the fond mothers could talk of nothing else. At some of these social gatherings, George overheard discussions on colours, styles and even the latest thing in underwear for the bright young things. The ladies of all ages went around in a fever of excitement and although the daughters of the house were still too young to take part in all this, they played at being débutantes.

Later in the year, the Orr Lewis family took their summer vacation in the South of France. They owned two villas there, both kept fully staffed, except for the valet and lady's maid, and their practice was to loan one of the villas to their close friends, Sir Montague and Lady Allen, and enjoy the holiday together. It was to be a real test of initiative for George, whose job it was to take charge of all the arrangements, the packing and checking, down to the last detail. He was even responsible for the passports and valuables, so he needed all his wits about him. Then, in the middle of it all, Duncan got himself into trouble again.

It was rag week for the colleges and the usual wild capers and carnivals were in progress. Though such high jinks were usually accepted, apparently Duncan had overstepped the mark and had climbed to the top of Eton College and placed a chamber pot on the spire. It proved to be a problem, since no one could think how to get it down, nor, indeed, how he had failed to break his neck getting it up there. Sir Frederick Orr Lewis was informed that expulsion was being considered. George witnessed fierce confrontation between Sir Frederick and Her Ladyship over the incident as she defended Duncan with all the excuses she could think of, but Sir Frederick was almost purple with rage, especially as he was faced with the bill of five hundred pounds to pay for damage and the services of the London fire brigade for retrieving the chamber pot. George heard all Duncan's previous sins well and truly aired, so he was apprehensive when, a few days later, he was instructed to take the car to Eton College to pack Duncan up and bring him home. Marshall drove George to the college in the Rolls, where he found his way to Duncan's room and knocked on the door. A voice from within yelled out,

'Come in, damn you, the door isn't locked.'

George entered to find a well-built young man in his

teens, sprawled on the bed. There was an untidy accumu-
lation strewn about the room and the place was thick
with cigarette smoke. The young man eyed George
sullenly as he explained his mission. Then he got off the
bed and inspected George from top to toe. 'So, you're the
old man's new flunkey, are you?' he said.

George remembered Sir Frederick's advice and decided
to treat Duncan like the spoilt brat he was. He began to
pick up some of the débris and Duncan watched him fold
them into a tidy pile on the bed.

'What's your name? I suppose you have got one?'

George still refused to rise to the bait and answered
quietly that his name was Slingsby, but that the family
preferred to call him George. He began to pack the things
into suitcases, sensing that Duncan was puzzled by his
calm attitude. Then he laughed.

'Right ho, George. You're not very talkative, are you?
Are you going to be my friend?'

George replied that it was entirely up to him and
Duncan laughed again.

'I see, they've got at you already. I suppose you've
heard what a bad lot I am? Is that it?'

George told him that he wasn't concerned with hear-
say and preferred to make his own judgment about such
things. Duncan was obviously disappointed that George
refused to be rattled and tried once more.

'All right, you cagey old bugger. I'll soon tame you.'

George paused in his task and looked him in the eye.

'That remains to be seen, doesn't it?' he replied.

After this, it seemed that Duncan had decided he had
met his match. On the journey home he was so amicable
that George could hardly believe this was the same arro-
gant young man whom he had first encountered. He
conversed in a sensible and friendly way and George
hoped that they may have found common ground.

Lady Orr Lewis greeted her son, literally, with open

arms. She cradled this well-proportioned youth as though he were a toddler.

'Dunkie, darling, Mamma is very glad to have you home.'

And Duncan played up for all he was worth.

All was now ready for the vacation departure the following day. Sir Frederick called George into his study that evening and gave him a few last-minute instructions and a small leather pouch containing a large sum of money in sovereigns and half sovereigns. He said this was the tipping purse and he advised George to be generous in this respect.

'Show these people the colour of your money, George, and you will find you get the best service.'

As soon as they began the journey, George discovered how true this was. Porters fell over one another to be of service and he felt like a millionaire as he doled out the pieces of gold. The luggage was whisked away to the quayside and, together with the two cars, it was taken on board. After this, he checked the passports and valuables into the purser's office and then joined the chauffeur in a well-earned beer.

George felt quite cock-a-hoop that everything had gone so well, but the sea trip was a short one, and in no time at all, he was repeating the procedure, this time through French customs. He was fascinated by the rapid chatter and wild gesticulations of the French all around him. Even the most casual conversation sounded like a heated argument, but everything went well. Where money was concerned, French porters seemed no different from those in England, and a sovereign from his tipping bag would work miracles. They hired a chauffeur to drive the Panhard, while Marshall took the Rolls, and they began their journey to the villa.

The beauty of the French Riviera surpassed anything

George had imagined. The immaculate gardens of the villas overflowed with exotic flowers and the white walls were festooned with wistaria and clematis. Boulevards were lined on either side with mimosa trees, and an early shower of rain brought forth the delightful perfume. He had often seen this lovely delicate flower in the baskets of the vendors in Piccadilly but hadn't realised it grew on such large trees.

Their arrival at the villa was also a new experience, for this was gentleman's service with a French flavour. As the cars drove up to the front door, all the staff were lined up to meet them in the usual way, but from then on there was no similarity to the routine of the English aristocracy. The butler, wearing a red carnation in his buttonhole and looking like the best man at a wedding, greeted Lady Orr Lewis and then led her along the line, like a general about to inspect his troops. It was the most curious assortment of staff that George had ever seen, starting with the housekeeper and three footmen, all of different sizes, about fourteen kitchen staff, three parlour maids, three chamber maids and a hall boy. Not one uniform appeared to match another, yet Her Ladyship seemed to find this quite acceptable. She greeted them all with the right amount of cordiality. Apart from the others, as though his dignity would not allow him alongside the underlings, stood the smallest man George had ever seen. He wore chef's overalls and his hat was very nearly as tall as he was. Lady Orr Lewis greeted him almost with affection. It was highly amusing to see this tiny man kissing the hand of the tall and stately lady. The whole scene was like a comic opera and George wanted to laugh. Later George learned why Her Ladyship had dished out such special treatment to this rather pompous little Frenchman who by reputation was acclaimed the finest chef in France, for this made her the envy of all her society friends.

Settling in took only a short time, for apart from the unpacking, the house was kept permanently in order. The staff may not have been orthodox by English standards but they were very efficient. Then George found himself faced with a problem. One of the pretty parlour maids took a fancy to him and didn't consider it at all indelicate to make amorous advances. Marshall thought it a great joke, but George was embarrassed by her behaviour. Her limited knowledge of English and his non-existent French made it difficult to tell her she was wasting her time, so he spent his time dodging her and hoping she would eventually get the message.

However, George did fall in love with the South of France, and his chance to see more of it came when the family received an invitation to dine with friends. Marshall drove the Rolls, with George in attendance, to a residence on the outskirts of Cannes, with instructions to return at midnight. Until then they were free to spend the evening as they pleased.

As soon as daylight faded, the water-front blazed with strings of coloured lights which illuminated the assortment of boats that bobbed at their moorings. They drove slowly along taking in the scene of French night-life. The hood of the car was down and a light breeze brought them the scent of flowers mixed with the tang of the sea. Music drifted from behind the walls that enclosed the private gardens. George was fascinated by the tables set outside the cafés, where candles in their glasses flickered romantically and beautiful women with their escorts sipped wine under striped umbrellas. It occurred to George that if people sat out on the pavements in England they would probably be arrested.

After a while, both men began to feel the need for refreshment, so they parked the car and took a seat at one of those outside tables. A waiter handed them a menu, but Marshall's smattering of French was not adequate to read it and their choice was made at random. Wine was brought automatically, but George never acquired a liking for French wines. He had a sweet tooth and they were all too dry for his taste. Indeed, to him what was served on this occasion was more like vinegar than wine. The meal, when it arrived, appeared to be the legs of a small chicken in aspic, served with a green salad and crusty French bread. George enjoyed every mouthful, but learned later that he had eaten his first frog's legs.

During the weeks that followed, George did his best to get to know more about the French and their way of life. He found them to be a curious mixture, loving one minute and ready to murder you the next. Food and love seemed to be second religion to them and some of their customs were strange to him. Prudity played little part in their lives. George got the shock of his life one afternoon when walking behind a young couple: the man suddenly stopped, exposed himself and urinated in the gutter. The young lady showed no surprise, and didn't even release her hold on his arm. French cigarettes and French beer were not to George's liking either, but he did adopt the Frenchman's way of smelling nice. Englishmen at this time considered it somewhat effeminate to smell of anything other than cigar smoke, but George decided to risk it and bought a number of different toilet waters.

The family spent much of their time entertaining, or being entertained. They visited the gambling casino at Monte Carlo, and joined friends for several weekends on a luxury yacht in the harbour. George saw some of the richest people in the world letting their hair down at the wildest parties. Then came the highlight of the holiday, the battle of flowers.

At the crack of dawn on the day of the procession, gay little barrows began to arrive, all piled high with carnival hats, masks and bunches of assorted flowers. Quite a number sold soft drinks and refreshments too, for it would be impossible to get service in any of the cafés or restaurants during the flower procession.

Sir Frederick and Lady Orr Lewis had a weekend engagement away from home, leaving George, Marshall and the lady's maid free until they returned. Her Ladyship insisted that the battle of flowers was an event that George should not miss on his first visit to France.

It was a hazardous journey getting through the streets of Cannes that morning and Marshall had to keep his wits about him as he drove the family to their destination. Already, the pavements were thronged with people seeking a spot where they could see the procession, and those who had found one were sitting tight. There wasn't a square inch of ground on which to stand comfortably by the time George and his two colleagues joined the masses; at first it seemed that all they were likely to see was the back of other people's heads, but then they noticed a high wall to one of the villas and decided it was a good place to stake their claim. With some difficulty, they hoisted the maid up first and then scrambled up themselves. Everyone carried armfuls of flowers, tied up into small bunches, and George too had bought several bunches of violets, even though he wasn't sure what to do with them. Then the procession began and everyone went mad with excitement.

The floats were magnificently decorated with the heads of thousands of flowers and some of the prettiest girls in France rode, smiling and tossing flowers to the crowd. To the blare of trumpets and the crashing of cymbals from every brass band in southern France, people returned the barrage, by hurling their bunches at the floats and at one another. Children danced along with garlands round their necks, banners waved and people cheered. Even the dogs joined in the fun, running alongside and barking their heads off.

The carnival queen and her attendants rode on the back

of a giant peacock made from flowers, its mechanical head nodding from side to side. Seated high up on a throne of golden marigolds, with the lovely tail of the peacock spread out behind her, the queen smiled and waved, while her attendants threw flowers from their baskets. George saw their blossoms dashed to pieces and trodden under foot. His own violets remained in his hand, for he had not the heart to see them suffer the same fate.

For almost two hours, float after float went by, each one more beautiful than the last, but as the procession passed, the crowds followed it, leaving the streets almost empty. The sun made George and Marshall realise that a cold drink and refreshment would be welcome and the two men jumped down from the wall. Getting the maid down, however, proved more difficult, for she was wearing the latest 'hobble skirt' – a slender tube from waist to ankles, which didn't allow much freedom for movement. Giggling, she was obliged to unbutton the skirt to above her knees before she could be lifted down safely.

❦ 12 ❧

Hostilities at Enfield

At the end of the holiday, George began to pack up for the return journey. He had made several small purchases within the limit of customs duty, but not so Her Ladyship. She had quite a number of things that would have to be declared, especially a very expensive hat by an exclusive Parisian designer. She had paid an enormous price for it, not only because the hat was a Paris model, but also because it was adorned with an osprey feather. There had been an outcry over the cruelty involved in curing these feathers, since the painful process had to be carried out while they were still attached to the live bird, so that they retained their beauty and stayed in perfect condition. To curtail the trade, a very high duty charge had been imposed.

George made a list of the dutiable articles, together

with an approximate estimate of payment to take them through customs and presented it to Her Ladyship who, he discovered, was not above doing a bit of smuggling for the sake of her precious hat.

'It's scandalous, George,' she exclaimed. 'They are thieves to charge duty at all, they do nothing to earn it. Pack it in with my other hats, they will never notice.'

George was surprised but did as he was told. She had paid fifty pounds for the hat and yet she was ready to risk the penalty for duty-dodging for the sake of paying just a little more. He later learned that Her Ladyship was a fairly regular offender in this respect.

Going through customs was quite an ordeal. George felt sure that guilt must show on his face. He declared his own small purchases, which were within the limit, and then the officer began to check the luggage. It was as though the man had X-ray eyes for, after chalking several pieces, he pounced on the hat-box.

'Open that one, please,' he said.

George did so, feeling prickles of alarm running up his back and, of course, the officer spotted the rogue feather at once.

George tried pleading ignorance, but the luggage was held, while he went in search of Lady Orr Lewis for further instructions. She was furious.

'I refuse to be brow-beaten. Tell them not to be so stupid. It's a blackbird's feather,' she said.

This absurd comparison failed to cut any ice with the customs man, who promptly confiscated the hat and gave a very stern warning that the consequences could be very serious if it should ever occur again.

Her Ladyship ranted and raved all the way home about the loss of her prized hat and they arrived back in London to weather that just about matched her mood. Grey skies and drizzling rain were not so pleasant after several weeks of glorious sunshine, but a message awaited Sir Frederick that brightened things considerably. It was from a house agent to say that a country residence at Enfield in Middlesex had come on the market and seemed suitable for Sir Frederick's requirements. The next day George accompanied his boss as they motored fifteen miles out of London to view White Webbs, set amid green fields.

The house stood at the end of a long drive in forty acres of park and woodland. It was a long, white building of about forty rooms, including servants' quarters, and had pleasant views from every window. There were also the usual outbuildings and stables. A generator brought water and light to the house and it seemed ideal. The immediate gardens were beautifully laid out and an ornamental lake supplied a shady retreat to the back of the house. Sir Frederick liked it, and Maples of London were called to do the furnishing. Shortly afterwards they moved in. The moment the paint was dry, Her Ladyship began to plan a house-warming party. This was the usual procedure for newcomers to the district, in order to know, and be known to, the appropriate circles. Colonel Sir Henry and Lady Bowles, whose estate adjoined White Webbs, headed the guest list, followed by Colonel Sir Alfred and Lady Somerset and Colonel Bosanquet. These were the prominent families in Enfield at that time, but many other dignitaries from farther afield were also added to the list.

George began to do a bit of socialising on his own account, beginning with a drink in the Rose and Crown, a small country pub just outside the gates of White Webbs. It was the sort of pub that was used as a meeting place, and it didn't take George long to become a favourite customer. Mr and Mrs Golding, the proprietors, were friendly people, and after George had dressed Sir Frederick for dinner, he would take a stroll through the park to find a small whisky and a friendly chat waiting for him there. One such evening, he was pleasantly surprised to be served by a very pretty girl, who was trying her skill with the beer pumps. It was the first time George had felt any real attraction for a member of the opposite sex, so naturally he set out to know her better.

She was introduced as Constance Lawrence, the eldest daughter of a close friend of the Goldings. The Lawrence family were well respected in Enfield, mainly through Mr Lawrence's work among the poor and sick of the district. He was a skilled cigar-maker for the Imperial Tobacco Company, and agitated for better conditions for his fellow employees, who laboured for a mere pittance. The years 1912 and 1913 brought really hard times for these people. Mr Lawrence was often called upon for help when a death occurred in a family whose financial status barely afforded bread for the living, let alone the expense of a funeral, and he would organise a concert to raise enough to bury the loved one. The Lawrences were just as benevolent with their hospitality too, and the time soon came when George was invited back to their home for supper. It proved to be a happy association with delightful people who, through their own talents, made their own entertainment at the piano in the parlour. These musical evenings were a source of delight to George and Mrs Lawrence's rabbit stew a great attraction.

Sir Frederick, however, discovered that another public house, situated at the other end of the park, was a meeting place for a very different clientele, the work-shy, poachers and those who lived by any other means of getting something for nothing. An unfenced foot-path ran between the adjacent estates of White Webbs and Forty Hall, the home of Colonel Sir Henry Bowles, to this notorious pub. It was a pleasant walk for those of good behaviour, but whenever a certain element was turned out with the saw-dust, there was trouble. Every Saturday night and Sunday lunch-time, drinkers wandered about the estate, coming close to the house, singing bawdy songs and generally causing an affray. Greenhouses and stables were broken into and the vegetable gardens pillaged. Sir Frederick complained to the police, but by the time they could reach the scene these people were always long gone. The situation finally exploded when a weekend house party was held at White Webbs for special friends.

There were about twenty guests and the younger ones of the party were spending their time out on the tennis courts, young ladies wearing the very latest fashions, which were considered rather daring since dresses had been shortened to calf-length, showing a saucy amount of leg. George was watching the fun from an upstairs window, when suddenly a group of unruly people came near the house. They were obviously the worse for drink, and they hung around the outside fencing making fun of those on the courts.

The butler was sent out to send them away, but this only provoked more abuse and the guests were driven off the courts to escape it. The young ladies were in tears and again the police were summoned to deal with these hooligans who constantly invaded their privacy. Lady Orr Lewis was angry and embarrassed and Sir Frederick vowed he would have the foot-path removed if it were the last thing he did. He consulted Colonel Bowles, whose estate also suffered from poaching and pilfering, and they joined forces to see what could be done.

They discovered the foot-path was a legal right of way and therefore could neither be closed nor moved. Some other way had to be found. The local newspapers had a field day, and made the most of the battle between rich and poor. The facts were distorted and the reports (although not inaccurate) made Sir Frederick sound the villain of the dispute. A certain set of well-meaning but misguided people took up the fight for what they called 'the working man's rights', and a lot of indignation flared up. People in small bands began to hang around the gates of White Webbs, carrying placards and shouting slogans such as 'Foreigner – go home', and 'Burn down the mansions and give our children bread.' Things about grinding the faces of the poor were chalked on the lodge walls and the wrought-iron gates were daubed with paint. Threats were made and stones were thrown at cars as they left the park – all of which only served to strengthen Sir Frederick's determination to fight on.

Finding efforts in that direction falling on stony ground, the campaigners then turned their attentions to the servants. A groom was waylaid at night and beaten up rather badly. George wasn't a coward by any means, but to be attacked in the dark, by more than one, was not his idea of fun. Sir Frederick even applied for a gun licence for defence. He then bought a revolver and, hearing George was losing his liberty to leave the safety of the estate on his evening off, applied for a second licence.

'We cannot allow these people to win with their threats of violence, George,' he said. 'You continue to meet your friends, but take the revolver with you for your protection.'

On these instructions, George set out to meet the Lawrences with the revolver tucked into his inside pocket. He spent a pleasant hour in their company, but had to decline their invitation to supper on this occasion because he was expected back at White Webbs. He left at about ten o'clock and started back through the park. There were no lights on the half-mile drive, which usually didn't bother George in the least. On this occasion he sensed that all was not well. He had a feeling he was being watched every step of the way and when he reached the part of the drive that ran through a clump of trees, he knew he was not mistaken. His trained country ear knew the difference between the sound of a nocturnal creature out in search of food and a human bent on mischief. He heard a dry stick snap under a clumsy foot and shone his torch in that direction. He saw a dark figure withdraw quickly behind a tree and held the light on the spot. Then he heard another movement from the other side and knew that if he didn't do something constructive, he would be getting the same treatment the groom had received. He took out the revolver and released the safety catch, then turned the torch back and forth between the sounds he had heard.

'I have a gun, and I'm prepared to use it if necessary,' he added.

There was complete silence. George pointed the gun at the sky and pulled the trigger. The report echoed into the night, and the next moment three dark shapes could be seen making a rapid exit towards the foot-path. George felt shaken, but the incident took effect. The demonstrations continued outside the gates, but were kept at a distance from the house.

This being so, Sir Frederick might well have dropped the whole proceedings. He was not a vindictive man and if these people were willing to keep the peace, that was all he asked. But then another incident occurred to make him renew his efforts.

When first he had taken up residence, he had made it known that the public would be allowed to pick up the sticks and fallen branches about the estate. He was well aware of the hardship among the genuine poor of the area and it was not unusual to see people gathering this free fuel. But one morning, when George was dressing Sir Frederick, the sound of sawing drew their attention. Sir Frederick knew he hadn't ordered any tree felling, yet from the window George could see several carts suspiciously lined up at the end of the drive. Sir Frederick put through a phone call to the lodge and sent the chauffeur to see what was going on. Five minutes later he learned that a party of men with two-handed saws had already cut down twenty young trees and even now were sawing them into convenient-sized logs and carting them away.

Sir Frederick was furious. The trees had been planted as a wind-break only a few years previously, and the men doing the sawing were members of the same idle set who had caused so much of the earlier trouble. The police were called and the logs confiscated, but as far as the young trees were concerned, the damage had been done.

'That is the thanks one gets for trying to be kind,' Sir Frederick stormed. 'They simply take it as a sign of weakness. Well, I am sorry to deprive the genuine ones, but the estate will be closed to the public in future.'

The dispute over the foot-path continued. It still couldn't be closed, but now that wilful damage to private property could be proved, Sir Frederick was allowed to fence it off – at his own expense. Since the foot-path was the dividing line between the two estates, Colonel Sir Henry Bowles agreed that each should foot the bill for his own side and the work began at once. The foot-path, known as 'the mile and a quarter alley', was duly fenced off on both sides with six-foot iron spiked railings, at the cost of something like £500, but both gentlemen were satisfied that justice had been done.

After this, life resumed a smoother passage, and Sir Frederick announced a trip to Canada. It was to be business combined with a visit to relatives and, of course, George's services were essential. Lady Orr Lewis decided a farewell dinner party for their closest friends would be nice and the preparations began.

Sir Montague and Lady Allen and their son Hugh arrived several days before the party and Sir Frederick immediately became anxious. Hugh Allen and Duncan were partners in mischief whenever they got together and the last thing he wanted was trouble before they sailed. He asked George in confidence if he would keep an eye on them during that evening, just in case they were hatching anything that could upset their plans.

It wasn't a job for which George would have volunteered, but if Sir Frederick wanted Duncan kept out of trouble, then that was what he had to do. He was valet to the two boys on the evening of the dinner party and felt like a traitor as he listened to their conversation. Most of it concerned young ladies of the theatre, and George knew that, on several occasions, Sir Frederick had had to pour oil on troubled waters when Duncan had made rash promises he had no intention of keeping. It was soon clear that they planned to slip out after dinner to meet two of these actresses, when two tickets for a London theatre fell out of Duncan's pocket.

All through dinner, the young men were on their best behaviour, but as the guests moved into the music room, they went into a huddle behind the potted palms. George saw them slip out through the French windows and creep round to the back stairs. George went via the main hall and was hidden in an anteroom when they came by. He heard Duncan say he had planted the car in a thicket some distance down the drive. While they changed into lounge suits, George hid himself in the shrubbery to await developments.

He knew it was no good appealing to their better nature about this; there had to be another way, if Sir Frederick's wishes were to be accomplished. He quickly decided that he would have to go with them. In due course two dim figures emerged, stealthily making for the hidden car. Once they were in the driver's seat, George quietly took the dicky seat on the back. He couldn't be seen for the folded top of the car, but he could overhear the conversation that went on as they started down the drive. If the two young actresses could have heard that conversation, they wouldn't have considered either to be gentlemen.

Reaching the gates they turned into the road. George popped his head over the shade and called, 'You might stop at the nearest post box, Duncan. I have a couple of letters to post for your father.'

Duncan slammed on the brakes and turned in amazement. 'What the bloody hell are you doing here?' he said. 'Get off and bugger off.'

George told him that it was his father's wish that he should not leave the house prior to sailing for Canada the next day. Duncan exploded.

'I see, the old man has appointed you chief watch-dog, has he? Well, we have an appointment, and we intend to keep it, so you can sling your bloody hook.'

George stuck his ground. 'All right – then we will all go,' he said.

Then came the abuse.

'You bloody old creeper,' Duncan stormed. 'Just because you're too bloody old, you think everyone else should be kept in a monastery.'

George, too old at twenty-four, grinned to himself in the darkness. He wasn't usually a kill-joy, but orders were orders. For several minutes, Duncan assailed him with every insult he could think of, but when this had no effect, he changed his tactics.

'Come on, be a sport, George,' he wheedled. 'It's not like you to be a snitcher. We won't stop out half the night. We promise to be back before midnight and they will never miss us, unless you open your mouth.'

George wanted to give in, but he knew their promises were as brittle as pie-crusts and he simply dare not risk it.

'I don't personally care what you do,' he told them, 'but your father wants you back at the house, and I shall be in trouble if you're not. Now be sensible, these young ladies will still be around when you return, and they will understand, I'm sure.'

Through the driving mirror, he saw the look and the

wink pass between the two boys, as Duncan appeared to capitulate.

'Oh, all right. They weren't up to the usual standard anyway. I'll drop you off to post those letters, and then we will go back to the fogie gathering.'

George knew exactly what they intended. The post box was on the corner of a cross-roads, and Duncan would have to slow down to turn the corner. George waited until the post box was in sight, hopped off before the car stopped, posted the letters and was back in his seat before they realised he had gone. Duncan stopped the car, and George called, 'I won't be a second.' This was Duncan's cue to put his foot down hard on the accelerator. He roared away, laughing.

'That's got rid of the nosy bugger,' he said.

George popped his head over the shade. 'All right, the letters are posted. We can go home now.'

Duncan almost choked with rage.

'You bloody leech. But right ho! I'll give you the roughest ride you have ever had.'

He was as good as his word, and drove like a madman over the roughest ground he could find, with George hanging on to his flimsy seat for dear life. The car bounced and bucked, as they careered over the pot-holes, and George's hands became trapped between the springs of the dicky seat. He dare not leave go for fear of being thrown off altogether, but every time the car bounced, the springs bit deeper into his flesh. The ride was a nightmare and it continued until Duncan's temper had subsided and they arrived back at the house. Never had George been so pleased to get his feet back on firm ground.

He went to his room to inspect the damage. Both his hands were cut and bleeding and one finger nail was partly torn off. He bathed them in salt water, but they were still sore and unsightly. He put on a pair of cotton gloves and poured himself a large whisky. He decided to say nothing to Sir Frederick in case it should cause the trouble he had tried to avoid, but as he turned the bed down that night, Sir Frederick noticed the blood that had soaked through the gloves.

'Good Lord, man, what have you done to your hands?' he asked.

George had to explain after all, and Sir Frederick was angry.

'Of all the brainless idiots, that boy takes the cake,' he said. 'If it were not for the fact that we sail in the morning, I would teach him a sharp lesson.'

He phoned the family doctor, who cleaned and patched George's hands with sticking plaster. Then, with a finger-stall over the torn nail, it felt much more comfortable.

The following morning George had no time to think about anything but the voyage ahead of them.

❧ 13 ❧
Winter in Canada

Most of the luggage had gone to the docks already, but there was still a lot to do before they finally went on board the *Mauretania*. Everything seemed to fall nicely into place, however, and they arrived at the quay in good time. George saw the great liner, towering majestically in her berth, and marvelled that anything so enormous could float. The family went straight to their cabins, leaving George to complete his list of duties before the eight-day voyage began. This done, George was then able to take in the bustling scene that is a prelude to the departure of any large ship. There were people milling about, some laughing, others tearful, all intermingled with the clatter of baggage being stowed away. He watched for a while before going to inspect his own cabin, which he was sharing with Duncan. After checking to see that everything needed during the voyage was there, he went back on deck again to watch the ship put to sea.

'All visitors ashore' was given for the last time over the loud-speakers, and George stood by the rails watching the last-minute comings and goings. People on the quay-side waved handkerchiefs to those on board. A deep note on the ship's siren echoed across the harbour. Then as the great ship shuddered and began to move, someone threw a coloured streamer, and then another, until the whole ship was festooned with them. It was a most thrilling experience, as the small tugs strained at the ropes to manoeuvre the giant out of the harbour. People cheered and waved as the gap widened between ship and shore. George leaned on the rails, taking it all in.

For the first three days at sea the weather remained perfect, and the passengers made the most of the amusements on board. The *Mauretania* was a floating palace that supplied only the best of everything and, after his duties, George explored to his heart's content. Then, on the fourth day out, the weather changed from warm sunshine to a stiff wind and choppy seas. The passengers discovered that racks had been fitted to the tables in the dining saloon, which indicated rough weather was expected. George had thought nothing could be worse than the storm during the crossing on the Irish ferry, but the rough sea in mid-Atlantic that night was terrifying. Dinner was a trial and many places were empty. As the storm worsened, port-holes were fastened and doors made secure. Passengers were warned not to venture out on deck and from then on it was difficult to keep upright. The huge liner tossed like a cork on mountainous waves the height of a church steeple. George managed to get Sir Frederick tucked up for the night and then climbed into his own bunk. Though not for long, for Duncan was suddenly seasick.

All through that night the storm raged and the ship pitched, tossed and rolled. They were on the crest of a giant wave one minute and down in a deep well of seething water the next. It seemed impossible for any ship to survive in such conditions, but through it all George was kept busy soothing Duncan and supplying him with small enamel basins. He had turned a sickly shade of green and was firmly convinced that he was dying.

Though George himself wasn't affected by sickness, nevertheless he was most relieved when, during the early hours, the storm began to subside. Duncan fell into an exhausted sleep and George gratefully crept into his bunk to snatch a little rest before resuming his duties. The sleeping accommodation of a double berth comprised one bunk above the other, and George had the top one. The ship had stopped tossing and had levelled out to a gentle rocking motion that soon lulled him off to sleep. Then one last big wave caused the ship to drop like a stone. George was lifted out of his bunk, to land with a crash that rattled every bone in his body. He lay, collecting his scattered wits and trying to get his breath, for the fall had winded him. Fortunately no permanent damage was done, but he finished off the night rolled up in his blankets on the floor, just in case fate had any more shocks in store.

By the next morning, brilliant sunshine and calm sea did much to restore the spirit. Even so, there were many who could not face breakfast. After serving Sir Frederick his, George took a turn round the deck to get some fresh air. The sunlight was catching the tips of the waves, and he watched the snowy wash against the ship's side. Not too far away, another young man seemed to be doing much the same thing and, on making his acquaintance, George discovered that he also was a valet. Over a cup of coffee in the sun lounge, they struck up a friendship that lasted for the duration of the voyage.

Other passengers were venturing out by this time, some still looking seedy, but among a group of people who entered the sun lounge was a lady George instantly recognised. It was Marie Lloyd, the musical comedy star, whose acquaintance he had made at a gala performance at Rufford. She spotted him too, and although she couldn't remember his name, she said she never forgot a face. More coffee was ordered, and Miss Lloyd promptly laced the pot with brandy from her personal flask, saying it killed the caffeine.

The rest of the voyage was spent in holiday mood, but by the seventh day, most were glad to sight land. Sea birds began to circle the ship as it passed the coast of Newfoundland, catching tit-bits thrown by those out on deck. George was determined not to miss anything of interest, and through the Cabot Strait and into the Gulf of the St Lawrence River, he began to feel excited at the thought of visiting Canada for the first time.

The *Mauretania* docked at Quebec earlier than was expected, despite the patch of rough weather, and George was plunged into the mad scramble through customs. He doled out his tips to an army of porters and issued orders like a field-marshall. Then with all the luggage safely through, the wagon-train proceeded to the station, where it was all loaded on to the train for Montreal. The giant locomotive, with a cow-catcher in front, belched steam and growled like some prehistoric monster. A bell clanged to call the passengers aboard. After seeing everything had been installed in the guard's van, George walked through the centre of several carriages until he found the family. He took a seat beside the lady's maid, next to the window.

'Everything all right, George?' Sir Frederick inquired.

'No trouble at all, sir,' George replied, feeling quite pleased with himself.

A whistle blew, a flag waved and the iron monster let out a roar. The last leg of the journey had begun and George's eyes were busy with the scenery through the carriage window. The brilliant autumn sunshine on the maple trees was a sight to behold, and George could well appreciate why the leaf of this tree had been adopted as Canada's emblem.

At Montreal station they were met by a chauffeured limousine, sent out by courtesy of the Hotel Metropole, and on their arrival, they were received like royalty. The hotel was the height of modern luxury and their every need was catered for. Central heating and air conditioning was a great improvement on many hotels George had known. Neon lighting was used more extensively here than in England too, and he was introduced to his first cocktail, the two coming together in the hotel bar. George watched fascinated, as the steward put his strange concoction together. A few drops of this and a dash of that, together with plenty of crushed ice, were put into a chrome shaker before the steward went into a frenzy of shaking movements. The liquid was then poured into a glass, decorated with mint, lemon or cherry, and given names such as 'Manhattan', 'Highball', 'Horse's neck' and 'Tom Collins'. George's opinion of these new drinks was favourable, but they were not very thirst-quenching.

There were other differences to the English way of life also, and one in particular proved a problem to George during the first few days. The staff used two languages, French and Canadian English, the latter employing rather odd turns of phrase. He was asked if he preferred his steak 'rare', which at first caused him to wonder if Canada had a meat shortage. He also discovered that Canadians held their trousers up with suspenders rather than braces. The word 'bum', which seemed to be widely used, was most confusing, until he learned that it described a person who, in England, would have been a tramp.

George's chance to see Canada came when Sir Frederick announced that he had business in a remote place called Rimouski, where he spent a lot of his time in conference, leaving George free to pursue his favourite hobby, getting to know people and places. 'Kelly's Eye' bar provided the opportunity for George to get into conversation with a man who was the tourist's delight. He seemed to be a walking guidebook on Canada and while George kept his glass filled he talked. At the end of all his information, he asked George if he would like to visit an Indian settlement and, of course, George said he would.

A streetcar took them to the edge of town, and there they began to walk over rough tracks and out into open country. Nothing was to be seen except miles of arid scrub-land, so that after half an hour George began to doubt the wisdom of allowing himself to be lured to such a remote place by a complete stranger. The uncomfortable thought that he could be robbed and left in this wilderness troubled him. However, over the next rise they came to a wire compound. At the gate, a large Government notice-board informed them of the regulations when visiting the Indian reservation. After passing through the gates, they continued to walk for some distance before they saw a cluster of colourful tepees, and dark-skinned children ran to meet them.

As a boy, George had collected a few leaden effigies of Indians, but to see them in real life, and in their own setting, was a great thrill. An old chief sat cross-legged outside his tepee, magnificently arrayed in his war bonnet of eagle's feathers. The deep lines etched on his face gave him a sculptured look and so motionless was he that

George wondered if he was real. But there was a lot of activity by the women of the tribe, stirring pots over open fires and generally going about their daily routine. Some were squatting on the ground making things in leather, while others wove and made lovely embroidery. George stopped to watch and smile at these decorative girls. Then his guide led him into a large tepee where all the work was laid out for inspection. A pretty Indian girl conducted him to a long table, where he saw fine examples of leather work from belts to moccasins. There were skin rugs, intricately carved figures in wood and strings of coloured beads, said to be a charm against the evil eye. At the far end of the tepee, several young girls were sewing shirts. The finished articles were laid out in rows; George lost his heart and a substantial sum from his wallet for a shirt of pure silk in the palest shade of lavender blue, with tiny pearl buttons. It was exquisite, and he thought the price – about five pounds in English money – was well worth the skilful work that had been put into it.

George noticed that, while he viewed the sale, his guide was in deep conversation with one of the elders of the settlement, and he suddenly realised why this man had been so eager to be helpful: he probably got commission from bringing custom to the Indians in this way.

Within the next two days the temperature in Rimouski dropped considerably. The Canadian winter had begun, and the journey back to Montreal took much longer due to heavy snow blocking the line. Although the train was heated, George had never been so cold in his life. He had thought Sir Frederick over-cautious when he had advised him to pack plenty of warm clothing, but now he was grateful. He hadn't realised that, in Canada, it could change from bright autumn weather to Arctic blizzard in a matter of hours. The train ran on a single track and, whenever another train approached from the opposite direction, one of them had to pull into a side-line to allow the other to pass. They were obliged to take part in just such a manoeuvre outside a place called Cucouna and were delayed for over an hour. It was cold and boring and the snow grew thicker all the time. George kept clearing the frost off the window to catch a glimpse of what was happening outside. On one occasion he thought he saw an Alsatian dog. He drew Sir Frederick's attention to it, fearing it had been stranded in the snow. In his ignorance, he was quite prepared to open the carriage door and take the dog into the warmth. At that very moment, the guard came through to warn people not to open doors or windows because the dog was a timber wolf out searching for food. George looked again and this time there were a dozen or more, prowling about under the train, and even begging up to the windows. It was an odd feeling to be nose to nose with a wolf, with only the thickness of glass between them.

Shortly afterwards they were able to proceed and the rest of the journey passed without incident. A car from the hotel was waiting at Montreal to whisk them back into the warmth of all that central heating.

It snowed all night, and next morning the sleighs were out. Montreal looked like a Christmas card, but it was extremely cold. Even his thickest clothing, adequate for an English winter, was virtually useless in these sub-zero temperatures. After breakfast, Sir Frederick sent out for an assortment of fur-lined overcoats, high-legged boots, ear muffs and fur hats. Thus, dressed up to look like a grizzly bear, George ventured out. Ploughs had piled the snow into high walls on either side of the street, with gaps left every few yards to allow pedestrians to cross. The sun was brilliant, but an icy wind made him walk quickly to keep his circulation going. The sleighs were most picturesque, as they went silently along, except for the little tinkling sound of bells on the horses' harness. Then the sun glinted on something less romantic. George noticed the frieze of icicles hanging from the gutters across the street. He looked up to see the same thing above him and instantly moved nearer to the edge of the pavement. He later learned that a great number of people were killed and injured every year when these icy daggers dropped suddenly. Icicles even hung from the nostrils of the waiting sleigh cab horses. By this time, George had had enough. He hurried back, feeling it would take him a week to thaw out. Before he reached the hotel, a man stopped him and pointed to his face.

'I say, fella, your nose is frozen,' he said.

George looked in the mirror down the side of a hairdresser's shop and saw that his nose was indeed bright blue.

'What do I do?' he asked the stranger.

'It's okay, buddy,' the man said with a grin. 'Just rub it with snow until the life comes back, but for God's sake don't go into the warm until it does, or your nose might drop off.'

He walked on, leaving George to follow his advice. The treatment worked, but painfully so. What George knew to be 'hot aches' in his fingers after playing in the snow when a boy, was now in the end of his nose. That night, despite the efficient central heating, he shivered in his bed. He added his overcoat to the bed covers for extra warmth, and before morning he even had the rug off the floor on the bed, but still he rose stiff and cold. Their visit was almost over and on this occasion George wasn't at all sorry.

Their return to England was later than Sir Frederick had planned, due to business commitments, so they spent Christmas on board the *Mauretania*. Only the bravest of souls ventured out on deck to face the icy wind. Instead, the passengers found their amusements inside looking out on to the beautiful, but marrow-chilling sight of the whole ship coated with ice from stem to stern.

However, Christmas at sea was anything but dull. Everyone had a wonderful time, dancing, dining and joining in the party games. There was a fancy dress ball on Christmas Eve for the adults and on Christmas morning they exchanged presents as usual. Duncan surprised George with the gift of a silk cravat. George held it up to himself for effect.

Duncan grinned. 'Oh, you're not a bad sort of chap, really, but if you ever split on me to the old man, I'll take the bugger back,' he said.

The *Mauretania* docked two days later. Winter had come to England as well as to Canada, yet it felt almost warm in comparison. Marshall was waiting with the car and warm rugs. The luggage was left to be sent by rail and they drove home to White Webbs and the comfort of blazing fires all over the house. George decided that central heating was fine, but nothing compared with a good coal and log fire.

George didn't get home to Babworth before February, then he took a week's leave. The snowdrops, planted by his father in the lawns, were in bloom, hundreds of them. There were fat buds ready to burst into spring foliage and the little bluetit had again built her nest in the letter box on the back gate. His family were delighted to see him home and the short holiday went all too quickly in renewing old acquaintances. Brother Arthur was still happy in the vineries of Rufford Abbey and had joined the Mansfield football club. Never much good on a dance floor, he was proving to be rather more nimble on the football field. Younger brother Alf was doing well in the St John Ambulance Brigade and was now called on duty at fair-grounds and local point-to-point races. He looked very grown-up in his uniform and white webbing. But apart from life moving on, the cottage, his parents and Babworth didn't change at all.

At the end of his leave, he returned to White Webbs in time for the annual rook shoot. Here was another event George could never quite agree with, especially as it took place in the nesting season. It was done to thin the birds out, of course, but it didn't seem right to George to shoot the parent birds and leave the fledgelings to starve. No such scruples were entertained by the guests who had gathered to take part in the shoot.

George had little time to ponder the iniquities, however, for he had his work cut out to cope with attending to guests in the party, among them Earl Castlemaine, a likeable gentleman who was always very generous over George's services. Whenever he visited White Webbs, George could be sure of a five pound note before he left.

The leaves crackled underfoot as the shooting party left the house. Duncan wore plusfours and a deerstalker hat. He looked the part, even if he was a rotten shot. George and the butler followed the party in the trap with a cold luncheon.

After hours of trailing through bushes and brambles, the shooters returned to the house covered in mud. George dumped the luncheon basket in the kitchen and resumed his normal duties, running baths for them all in turn. He settled Sir Frederick among the suds and then went to attend to Earl Castlemaine. This gentleman was rather eccentric in many ways and George was acquainted with most of his foibles. For example, he had his suits hand-made by an exclusive tailor and yet his underpants always looked as though he had been peppered with buckshot. There was more darning wool in his underclothes than original material! George concluded that, with his great wealth, he could afford to be eccentric. He helped the Earl peel off his mud-stained togs and then began to run his bath, noticing as he did so that there was a bottle of Jameson's three-star brandy on the ledge by the bath. He knew the Earl enjoyed this particular brand, but had never known him before to indulge while bathing. The gentleman's voice cut across his thoughts, as he called out from the dressing room.

'You will find a bottle of brandy in there, George, put it in the bath water, there's a good chap.'

George thought it odd but did as he was told, then helped the Earl to lower his long frame into the bath. He explained to George that brandy used in this way was the finest thing out for preventing aches and pains after being out in the weather.

'Keeps the rheumatics away better than that foul-smelling liniment,' he said.

It seemed to George a shocking waste of good brandy, as he left the Earl to soak while he went back to dress Sir Frederick.

A quarter of an hour later he went back to Earl Castlemaine, who was singing snatches of an Irish folk song. As he opened the bathroom door, the fumes from the brandy in the hot water almost overpowered him. It was enough to make anyone tipsy, just breathing them in. He helped the Earl out and wrapped him in a bath towel, then he pulled out the plug and watched all that brandy go down the drain. George had to admit it cleaned the bath nicely, and probably sterilised the drains too.

❦ 14 ❧
George in Love

As George's friendship with the Lawrence family progressed he spent more and more of his free time in their company. He was almost considered to be one of the family and he and the son Pete had become good pals. The daughters were all pretty and full of fun, but Connie, who had been George's fancy from their very first meeting, already had a young man and George was too honourable to poach on another man's preserves. They did, however, continue to be partners for the occasional dance at the local church hall. Both were excellent dancers and, since most of the family would also attend, their association became happily platonic.

There was one member of the family who was very pleased about this state of affairs, Connie's younger sister, Dorothy, who had lost her heart to George from the first moment they met. She wasn't an accomplished dancer, which would have brought her into closer social contact with the man of her dreams, but she did stand out a little from her other attractive sisters whenever her father coaxed her to sing for the family entertainment. Dorothy did possess a lovely voice and George, having been top choir boy of four counties, appreciated her talent, and it was listening to her singing such love songs as 'Thora' that finally kindled the spark between them. In time a closer acquaintance grew, and with Mr Lawrence's approval, it became accepted that George and Dorothy were 'walking out'.

When George had been courting Dorothy for twelve months, it became accepted with the Lawrences that they would eventually marry. George's family were not so well informed. His mother, at any rate, always hoped that he would choose a nice local girl when the time came. She meant no disrespect to Dorothy, but firmly believed that country people should marry country people. Dorothy, however, was George's choice and he decided to take her to meet his family before buying the engagement ring.

Romance was already in the air at Babworth, with the wedding of 'Young Master Jackie' Whitaker. The marriage took place at the Guards' Chapel in London and after a champagne lunch with his brother officers, the couple came home to the wedding breakfast at Babworth Hall. It was November, but mild for the time of year and a large marquee was erected in the park, where refreshments were provided for the estate employees to join in the celebrations. It was Dorothy's first look at life on a gentleman's estate and she was acutely aware of being under scrutiny as George's young lady. They made her very welcome, but George realised that it would take time for both to adapt.

Another special happening occurred when the 'gipsy

pike' was caught during an angling contest in Babworth
Lake. George was showing Dorothy around and talking
to the fishermen when a commotion on the other side of
the lake drew their attention. They sprinted across the
rustic bridge to join the excited men who were struggling
with an enormous fish. The shark-like jaws snapped
viciously as it was drawn up the bank with great care.
It brought back a boyhood memory for George as he
explained to Dorothy why this fish was different from
any other. Twenty years previously, a band of gipsies,
travelling through Retford, had been delayed when one
of the women had become seriously ill. They were com-
pelled to stop to save the woman's life, but in those days
vagrancy was punishable by a term of imprisonment.
They sought help at Babworth Hall and Sir Albert had
been most concerned. He allowed them to camp in the
park, supplied them with milk and vegetables and gave
them access to fresh water. He even offered to call the
services of his own doctor, but they preferred to use their
own remedies.

The painted caravan and the gipsies had fascinated the
children of the estate. George remembered hiding among
the rhododendrons above the lea where the caravan was
parked, watching them tending an iron pot hung over an
open fire. They had stayed until the woman was fully
recovered then, for Sir Albert's consideration, they presented him with a young pike with a small silver ring in
its lip. This was put into the lake with a gipsy blessing
that, as long as the fish remained, prosperity would pre-
vail. Consequently, each time the pike was caught, it was
recorded and carefully returned to the water.

They watched now as the pike was weighed. Seeing
the fight between men and fish, Dorothy kept her distance. The man sent to notify Sir Albert returned rolling
a barrel of ale, which was tapped off into the fishermen's
mugs. Then the pike was unwrapped from the sack in

which it had been held, and lowered into the water. It was quiet for a moment, then shot off into the weeds. The fun was over for that occasion.

On their return to Enfield, the engagement ring was bought and a small celebration was held at the Lawrences' home. No date was made for the wedding then, mainly due to George's profession. Dorothy understood the ruling and was content to wait, hoping that when the time came, Sir Frederick would allow them to occupy one of the lodges and George to continue in his employment.

The spring brought preparations for the Orr Lewis family's usual holiday in the south of France which was generally taken in the company of their great friends, Sir Montague and Lady Allen, who usually arrived at White Webbs a week before they were due to sail. After dinner one evening, the bell rang to summon George, who went into the dining room to find a rather odd atmosphere prevailing: Lady Orr Lewis was obviously hesitant about something, while Lady Allen sat with the adored little Pekingese she called Peek-a-boo on her lap, a strange expression on her face.

'George, I am going to ask you to do us the most tremendous favour,' Lady Orr Lewis began. 'It is apart from your usual duties, so I shall understand if you feel you could not accept the responsibility.'

George's imagination ran riot. Then Lady Allen took over.

'It's Peek-a-boo, I simply cannot find anyone I could trust well enough to take care of him while I'm away. I'm at my wit's end to know what to do for the best.'

'Perhaps a good kennel would be the answer, madam?' George suggested, but she held up her hands in horror.

'Oh! no, George,' she exclaimed. 'I left him to their tender mercies once before and the poor darling almost starved to death. He simply wouldn't eat a thing because he was parted from me, so that is quite out of the question.'

He waited for her to come to the point, and she did.

'I am wondering if it is possible for you to smuggle him through customs? I just know you could do it and I would be so grateful. So would Peek-a-boo, wouldn't you, darling?' She gave the dog a hug, while George's hair nearly stood on end.

'How do you propose to do this, madam?' he said as calmly as he could.

'Oh! I haven't the slightest idea, George,' she replied. 'I'd leave it all to you, you are so clever at managing these things.'

Four pairs of eyes were focused on him, waiting for his answer and he couldn't think of any way of wriggling out of the situation. Reluctantly he agreed to think of something, and Lady Allen was jubilant.

'I knew you wouldn't let us down, George. Whatever should we do without you?'

At the moment he had no idea in his head of how this venture was to be carried out and told them he would need time to think about it. Well, he had been warned that to be the perfect valet one had to accomplish the impossible, but he hadn't anticipated placing himself on the wrong side of the law. Now the die was cast, and he was faced with the task of saving Peek-a-boo from six months in quarantine.

In the confines of his own room, George racked his brains for a plan that wouldn't end with them all under arrest. With a diamond, or something small, it would have been bad enough, but what on earth did one do with a dog?

Then an idea began to form. He had always found that the more simple the method, the more chance of success, but to carry out his plan, he would require Lady Allen's help. First, she would need to find a vet willing to pre-scribe a sedative to keep the dog asleep long enough to get them safely into France. Then, if he carried it in a small lunch basket, with a car rug over his arm to hide it, he might get away with it undetected.

The next morning, he outlined his plan to Her Lady-ship, who beamed her admiration.

'George, you're a genius,' she said. 'I do have a good vet and I'm sure he will be sympathetic to our cause.'

She ordered the car at once and set out for London with the little dog on her lap, returning later with the sedative and instructions on how it should be administered. All they needed now was a lot of luck.

The morning of their departure arrived and the two cars stood waiting to take them to Dover. Lady Allen was fussing like an old hen, for now the time had come to put their plan into action she was all nerves in case something went wrong. Even though she had been assured that only Britain quarantined animals coming in from abroad, she insisted on smuggling the dog out of the country too, reasoning that the animal could be noticed and remem-bered at Dover on the way out and looked for on their return. The little dog travelled most of the way on her lap. She had delayed his breakfast of minced chicken so that he would readily take the sedative when the time came. It was timed almost like a military operation: the cars stopped just before they reached the docks and the knock-out drops were fed to Peek-a-boo, with Lady Allen wailing, 'Oh, I do hope it doesn't taste nasty.'

Judging by the way it was bolted, George rather doubted whether he even tasted the chicken. Then Lady Allen nursed the little dog until he went to sleep. George took over then, putting Peek-a-boo into the basket and strapping the lid down. Then they continued on their way. But just before they reached the dockside, a compli-cation set in: the dog began to snore. This was something they hadn't anticipated and, with the flattened nose sounding like a saw mill, the customs man would have to be stone deaf not to hear it. Something had to be done, and quickly. George opened the basket and very gently moved the dog's position; to their relief, the snoring stopped.

They eventually arrived without further trouble and George, with the car rug placed over the basket on his arm, made for the customs shed. The officer on duty greeted him cordially, exchanged a few pleasantries as the baggage was checked, then rattling his tipping bag significantly, George rounded up an army of porters and followed the laden trollies out into the sunshine. Lady Allen, watching from the ship's rails with anxious eyes, caught George's guarded signal and almost collapsed with relief. Even so, there was the same nerve-racking procedure to face when they docked in France.

George sat out on deck, with the basket on his lap, for the short sea passage. Several people looked at him strangely, to see him cuddling a car rug on such a warm day, but just in case the snoring started again, he dare not be where others could hear. As it happened, luck was with him; he cleared the French customs without incident and, once the cars were unloaded, they began their journey to Nice. George sat up front with the chauffeur where he could enjoy the scenery. Before they had gone very far, a series of snorts and snuffles indicated that Peek-a-boo was waking up. They stopped the cars and opened the basket to find a very bewildered and bad-tempered little dog which, apart from a slight watering of the eyes, seemed no worse for his adventure.

The scenery changed as they motored further south. Palm trees grew all along the coast road and the walls and gardens of the villas blazed with colour. There was a tropical look about everything here, with the trees dressed for summer. A tranquil blue sea gently rocked the luxurious boats moored in the harbour and George began to feel the difference in temperature too. Then suddenly they turned into the imposing gates of Villa Edelweiss and drove to the house through a rustic archway, where laburnum trees had been trained to let their golden trails hang through. The effect was quite beautiful as this enchanting tunnel opened out to large stretches of velvety lawns and colourful flower beds, right up to the front door. The villa gleamed white in the bright sunlight, its window boxes overflowing with perfume and colour. A wide veranda and the terraces were covered with wistaria and a large ornamental lake, with water-lilies the size of dinner plates, looked cool and inviting. A green dolphin spewed a plume of sparkling water at one end, and the statue of a little girl dipping her toes under a large willow stood at the other. There was a long sun-lounge, with pink flagstones, that led through rose gardens and down to a private beach.

Once again the family spent a lot of their time away from the villa, dining, dancing and gambling, leaving George to explore the fifteen acres of orange and lemon groves attached to the grounds, a cool and fragrant place to sit on a hot day. Then one evening, before a dinner party, Lady Orr Lewis complained of a bad headache. She rested in a darkened room, but an hour later her condition had worsened and her throat had become very sore. The doctor was called and diphtheria was diagnosed. Lady Orr Lewis was taken at once into an isolation hospital.

It appeared that an epidemic had broken out around the dock area of Marseilles and it was feared that a carrier had brought it into France about the same time they had arrived. The doctor proceeded to take swabs from every person in the house. It was explained that a 'carrier' need not necessarily have the disease, but could spread the germ without knowing it. Unless this person could be found, it would be impossible to stop the epidemic.

The guests were cancelled and dinner that evening was a gloomy affair. Sir Frederick scarcely left the phone in case he should be needed urgently, and it was as if a pall had been cast over the whole house.

The following morning, however, George was in for a shock. The report on Her Ladyship was that a tracheotomy had been performed and, although she was still seriously ill, she was considered out of danger. Then the health authorities arrived and George listened with horror as they explained that his swab had been positive. Because he showed no signs of being ill, he was suspected of being the carrier.

He felt stunned and unclean as he watched all his clothes being removed for fumigation, then he too was taken into isolation. He was told that he would be kept completely out of contact with other people while tests were carried out to determine whether he was indeed the carrier. How long all this would take, they couldn't say. He had no idea of his destination as he was taken off by ambulance, but after what seemed a very long journey they arrived at a large prefabricated construction with a corrugated iron roof. George mentally named it 'the tabernacle'. There wasn't another building in sight and no sign of life inside the tabernacle either. It was in need of a coat of paint, George noticed, and the grounds were neglected. He felt like a convict.

Inside, the building turned out to be quite habitable. It was well furnished and there seemed to be everything for his needs. He was told he could use the phone as often as he liked and that a nurse would come to him three times a day to bring food and to take tests. A doctor would also visit him every day to check his state of health. Then, having made sure he was settled in, the ambulance party departed.

For the first few hours, the situation wasn't too bad.

He acquainted himself with every inch of the house, then went out into the sunshine to explore the grounds until the nurse came to bring him his first meal in solitary confinement. But as darkness fell, the reality of his position struck home. The significance of being a carrier closed in on him, as he sat alone with a bottle of whisky. It wasn't a pleasant thought, to be an outcast from society. He thought of his family, and of Dorothy, who was wearing his ring and stitching her trousseau, and the more he thought, the more he drank, until he staggered to bed to sleep like a log.

The next morning, he awoke with an appalling head-ache and couldn't face breakfast. The nurse prattled on cheerfully in French, took another swab, patted his arm sympathetically and left. He had been told he could write letters, but they too had to be fumigated before they were posted. He wanted to share his fate with someone, but he saw no kindness in distressing his loved ones at this stage, so he sat down to write a cheerful 'wish you were here' type of letter. It was difficult to write about the beautiful south of France when he really felt as miserable as sin, but he did his best to sound as though he were having the time of his life. Then he phoned the villa to inquire about Lady Orr Lewis's condition and was relieved to hear that she was making satisfactory progress. Sir Frederick told George that he was not to hesitate to ask for anything he needed to help make the situation more bearable. Then, after the receiver was replaced, George was left to face another day of sheer boredom.

They do say one can become used to anything, given time, and George certainly had plenty of that. He looked forward to seeing the little nurse pop in and found amusement in trying to work out a set pattern of signs to make her understand him. She, too, seemed to get fun out of his deaf and dumb language and would leave him laughing like anything. From time to time, members of the household phoned him and Marshall, the chauffeur, was always a welcome voice on the other end of the line. He nearly always had some snippet of news to brighten George's day, but the phone call that surprised him most came from Duncan. George was rather touched.

'Hello, George – you old bugger. I hear they've got you nicely caged up. I always said you would look better behind bars.'

Not the most cheerful message, you might think, but George knew Duncan's warped sense of humour. It was his way of letting George know that he cared.

The six weeks of isolation were the longest weeks in George's life. Then he was told that the real carrier had been found. On reflection, it seemed ironical that he had taken so much risk in saving the little dog from the same fate. After six weeks in quarantine himself, he felt almost justified in having saved Peek-a-boo from being parted from his beloved mistress for six months.

The Rolls arrived to fetch him home in style and the welcome he received was almost more than his sentimental nature could bear. Lady Orr Lewis was now out of hospital, but still convalescent, and George was eager to get back into his routine. In the next few days, he got his wish. Everything that Sir Frederick owned looked as though it had come out of the rag bag. His suits were unpressed, his underclothes soiled and his socks undarned. Buttons were missing from everything and cufflinks that were thought to be lost turned up in shirt sleeves that had lain in the dirty linen basket since George had been carted away. Now he had to set to work to put it all in order.

The Orr Lewises had, of course, extended their stay in France because of Her Ladyship's illness, but Lady Allen had delayed their return for the sake of getting her dog back to England. George wondered what she would have done if, in fact, he had been the carrier. Knowing her fondness for her pet, she would probably have made her home in France, rather than give him up.

A dinner party was arranged to celebrate Her Ladyship's recovery and most of the smart society set were on the guest list. The bumptious, pint-sized chef was in the kitchen, creating his masterpieces and still enjoying his importance. Lady Orr Lewis boasted that he made the most perfect consommé in the whole of France and her smart friends agreed with her. Even George had to admit the fellow knew his stuff, despite being a detestable little dictator. He sent the menu for Her Ladyship's approval, which she did, and George was asked to return it with her compliments. It wasn't usually George's job to do this, so he didn't come in contact with the chef very often. Now he entered the holy of holies. He had never seen anything like it. It was more like a parade-ground than a kitchen, with the cocky little chef as sergeant-major. He rapped out orders at the top of his voice, while the kitchen staff hopped about like scalded cats. There were fifteen of them, all going at top speed. The under-chef was walloping the daylights out of a piece of meat with a wooden spatula, while others were chopping, stirring and blending as if their lives depended on it. And, all the time, 'King pin' waved his arms and tapped them on the head with a wooden spoon whenever he considered they needed rousing. Then his eye fell on George and his goatee beard quivered with indignation. He approached slowly and drew himself to his full height, which was just level with George's shoulder, and fixed him with a withering look.

'What are you doing in my kitchen?' he snarled.

George quietly explained his mission and handed him the approved menu. A sarcastic smile spread over the chef's face.

'So, Zey send me ze errand boy,' he sneered, and began to walk round George, looking him over in an insulting way. His breath stank of garlic, which he constantly chewed, and George was very tempted to push that silly hat down over his eyes. He may have been prized above rubies to the upper set, but to George, he was just an objectionable little man. For several seconds they stared at one another, then, when this self-styled Napoleon decided he had brought George to heel, he turned rudely away and began to stir a large stock pot that was kept constantly simmering on the range. He added a few scraps that George wouldn't have given to a dog to the already curious assortment, including egg shells floating round on top. This was presumably the mixture that eventually became the celebrated consommé soup. George could scarcely believe his eyes when the little chef cleared his throat before replacing the lid and spat into the pot. This was too much, when George knew he had eaten this man's food.

'You dirty bugger,' he exclaimed. 'If I had my way, I'd sack you on the spot.'

The chef looked amazed that anyone should dare to speak to him in this way. His eyes rolled, his face went scarlet with rage and flecks of foam appeared at the corners of his mouth. Then he exploded.

'You dare to insult me in my kitchen! You – you – nobody, you peasant, you whippersnapper – you – '

He ran out of words and made a grab for a large meat cleaver. As the little man advanced menacingly George decided it was time to leave. Just as he slipped through the door, the chef threw the cleaver as hard as he could. It hit the door as George closed it behind him, to screams of '*Allez-vous en*'.

George's first impulse was to go straight to Her Ladyship, but knowing how she prized her much sought-after chef, he doubted whether she would believe him. It would be his word against the chef's shining reputation, and George felt he had had enough trouble recently, without going into battle with a status symbol. He simply decided that from now on, he would avoid consommé soup at all costs.

Two weeks later they left the south of France. George, once again, put the sedated Peek-a-boo into the basket, feeling this time almost virtuous as he made for the customs. The luggage went through without a hitch and the dog slept soundly all the way to Dover. Then, as the boat was about to dock, loud snores began to come from under the rug over his arm. People nearby began to look at him curiously and it was clear something had to be done. He went into the toilets and unfastened the basket, but this time he had to move the little dog several times before the snoring stopped. All he could do now was to pray that he would sleep quietly for the next half hour.

Then came the procedure of gathering porters to deal with the luggage and he followed them into customs. The long line of people seemed to move more slowly than usual, with George on pins at every step. Just three spaces away from the checking table, the dreaded snoring began again. George shuffled his feet, blew his nose and rustled the newspaper he was carrying, hoping to detract from that terrible sound. At the moment no one seemed to notice for the noise of the general activity around them, but it was too much to hope that the sharp-witted customs officer wouldn't hear it. He slid his hand under the rug and gave the basket a shake, but the snoring continued. In desperation, he almost turned the basket upside down and to his relief there was one loud snort and then silence. He cleared customs without trouble but silently vowed that nothing would induce him to do this again.

After another short business trip to Canada the Orr Lewises gave a dinner party at White Webbs, on which occasion George was in for a lovely surprise. Lady Allen was there as a house guest, and after dinner was over and the guests had gone, the bell summoned George to the drawing room. Lady Allen, all smiles, handed him a small package.

'This is for you, George,' she said.

Inside was a small leather box with a card that read

With our grateful thanks, from Peek-a-boo and me

Lady Allen.

He lifted the lid to see a diamond tie-pin in the shape of a horseshoe, and for a moment felt lost for words. He had not expected any reward for taking the little dog through customs, but this showed that his services above and beyond the call of duty were appreciated. He thanked her and proudly pinned it on to his tie. On his next visit to the Lawrences, brother Pete made a lot of fun at George's expense. He wagged a warning finger playfully.

'Blimey, George, if you go on like that you will get yourself a bad name,' he said.

❦ 15 ❧
Discovering America

George's next voyage was to the United States and, this time, it was to be a combination of business and pleasure for the Orr Lewises and the Montague Allens. A week before they were due to sail, George was called into the drawing room and offered a glass of sherry. His heart sank, suspecting there was more to the gesture than met the eye, and he was right. Lady Orr Lewis explained that they had just discovered that jewellery worth over a certain amount was liable to customs duty. This posed a problem for both ladies, since they wished to take most of theirs with them to America.

'It's ridiculous, George,' she said indignantly, 'to expect anyone to pay duty on one's own jewellery. It is taking liberties. It's not as though it were new. Some of it has been in the family for generations.'

Lady Allen backed her up.

'You see, George, we are committed to attend some very important functions. I should feel positively naked in society without a few pieces.'

George could see what was coming, but as he looked from one to the other, he knew he was in a cleft stick. Having taken it for granted that he would do their bidding, they produced their baubles and George tried not to show the alarm he felt. He had expected just a few of their best pieces, but when they produced something in the region of £40,000's worth between them, he almost had a fit. There were tiaras, brooches, bracelets and necklaces, and, in the background of his thoughts, he heard Lady Allen saying, 'We know you can do it, George, you're so clever at these things.'

The horrible answer to that was he wouldn't be so clever if he should be caught with that lot.

In the privacy of his own room, he searched his mind for a good idea. There was so much of it! Where on earth did they expect him to hide it all? It had to be somewhere about his person, because he dare not let it out of his keeping, but it also had to be in a place that gave him freedom of movement. After grappling with the problem half the night, he had the only solution he could think of by morning.

As soon as breakfast was over, he sent out for a wide roll of cotton wool and a crêpe bandage of equal width. Then he had a trial run. He stripped and put a layer of cotton wool round his waist, next to his skin. Next he threaded the jewellery on to a strong cord, spacing the pieces out according to shape and size, and tied it like a belt over the cotton wool. Then, with another layer of cotton wool over that, he bound himself with the crêpe bandage. It took a bit of practice before it was comfortable and yet tight enough not to allow his precious cargo to shift. He tried a series of bending and stretching movements to make sure everything was secure, then put on a thick under-vest and dressed himself in the usual way. After this, he looked in the mirror and felt fairly confident.

The day of departure came and the party was installed in the two cars, with George riding next to Marshall in the Rolls. As he climbed in, the chauffeur shook his confidence a little by remarking, 'Blimey, George, either you've put on weight, or that suit has shrunk. It's no good mate, you'll just have to cut out the beer.'

George grinned, but said nothing. The fewer people who knew his secret the better. He reasoned that Marshall knew him well and saw him every day, but strangers in the confusion of a busy dock would not be likely to notice that his waist was several inches thicker than it ought to be. Anyway, it was too late to alter things now.

On the long journey, the hot August sun made the thick padding feel like horsehair. It prickled and itched, until he longed to open his shirt to let some cool air in. Marshall still kept giving him some curious glances, but at last they reached their destination, and after that there wasn't too much time to think about it.

With the usual entourage of porters, he followed them into customs. If ever George was called upon to keep his head, it was now, facing that sharp-eyed customs man with the equivalent of half the crown jewels on a string round his waist. But there were no complications. The luggage was checked, the officer wished him 'bon voyage' and he was through. He followed the porters with their laden trollies out on to the quayside, where the cool breeze did much to restore his flustered feelings.

The *Mauretania* waited majestically, with the sunlight glinting on the superstructure. She had carried George and Sir Frederick to Canada previously, but now she had been put on a shuttle service with her sister ship the

Discovering America

Lusitania to and from the United States. George watched the luggage going aboard and the cranes lowering it into the belly of the ship, then joined the throng of jostling people to check the passports. The family were already on board. Until the giant ship sailed, George's work was done. He made a bee-line for the nearest bar for a cool beer and to watch the activity that never failed to excite him before a voyage. Half an hour later the ship shuddered and loud speakers bellowed 'All visitors ashore', gangways were removed and, amid cheers and a sea of fluttering handkerchiefs, the *Mauretania* got under way. Coloured streamers were thrown from the rails and trailed on the breeze as the ship moved away from the quay.

The jewellery belt by this time was becoming a real torture. George felt that if he didn't get it off soon he'd be scarred for life. He went to his cabin, stripped off and took a bath. Then he dressed again with more care, discarding the thick winter vest, and felt more comfortable after that.

The voyage was the usual holiday at sea, with marvellous food and good entertainment. A school of dolphins delighted the children on board by giving a spirited display of acrobatics round the ship, and fine weather followed them all the way to New York, when again, George had to dress with care. He joined the queue for the customs with his mountain of baggage in time to witness a disturbance. People craned their necks to see a struggle by several policemen to apprehend a man who was led away in handcuffs. As George neared the checking table, it didn't help his conscience to hear a customs officer remark, 'He hasn't had a bad run, we've been looking for him for a long time.' Apparently the man had been smuggling diamonds. The contraband round George's waist seemed to burn into his flesh and he hoped he didn't look as guilty as he felt when he faced

153

that same officer. But the luggage went through, and George got himself quickly out of there.

The larger pieces of luggage were left for later collection. The rest was piled on to a fleet of cabs that followed their own car like a convoy. George had bought a guide book to the United States, but the real thing still surprised him and surpassed anything he had imagined. The height of the skyscrapers astounded him, and he wondered however they stayed up in a high wind. Everything flashed with neon lights. Elaborate moving adverts blazed everywhere, and although he had seen this to some extent in London and Canada, he had to admit nothing compared with this. Electric lighting of any kind was comparatively new in England, where most illumination was still by gaslight and in many of the more remote places, people still relied on oil lamps. He was fascinated by two neon clowns who threw a ball back and forth to one another, and a windmill rotated its sails in all the colours of the rainbow.

The motorcade stopped outside the Hotel Ritz Carlton and an elaborately decorated commissionaire stepped forward with a smart salute. A chain of bell hops whisked the luggage away to the suites of rooms, as the entourage entered into a world of chromium plate and more neon lights. An express elevator took them up to the 29th storey at such a speed that George supposed one collected one's stomach on the way down.

By now, George's only desire was to be rid of his penance belt, but first he made sure the family were settled for the next half an hour, then he went to his own room and stripped off. A line of dents round his waist irritated so much that he stood like an old woman who had shed her tight corsets and had a good scratch. After soaking himself in the bath, he dressed again and took the jewellery to the ladies, who were full of praise for his effort.

'George, you are a treasure,' Lady Allen chuckled. 'If you were not such an excellent valet, you could make a fortune as a smuggler.'

George respectfully told her that he would never stand the strain.

As soon as the opportunity was presented, George went out to explore New York. He had plenty of free time, since most services were carried out by the extremely efficient hotel staff. In fact, there were times when he felt almost redundant, with so many of his duties taken over. The management were quite astonished when Sir Frederick objected to a pert young maid running his bath. George chuckled while dressing his boss one morning to hear him explain, 'Damn it, George, I can't have a young woman popping in and out of my bathroom. Her Ladyship would play the devil.'

As always, George went to the hotel bar for his information. He sipped a drink called 'scotch on the rocks' and listened to the barman's glowing description of Central Park and the tallest building, which was, at that time, the Woolworth building. Then, on his free day, he sallied forth into the streets of New York. The traffic was one continuous stream of clanking streetcars and every other sort of vehicle one could think of and in the middle of it all stood a lone policeman, with a revolver at his hip. He conducted the traffic with the biggest baton George had ever seen and George stood for a while watching the activity. Then he just sauntered along, looking and learning. It was a sweltering hot day, the heat from the pavements burned through the soles of his shoes and he could feel the perspiration trickling down his back. A neon sign announcing 'Beer parlour' was like an oasis to a thirsty man. He went in to find the establishment was rather like the Canadian equivalent, except that here they admitted women.

As soon as he took a stool at the bar, the net began to

close. Two gaudily dressed girls approached, smiling
sweetly, and one asked if he would like to buy two thirsty
girls a drink. George smiled back, but the barman at the
hotel had warned him that an unsuspecting customer
could be made to pay through the nose for nothing more
than coloured water. These places were known as 'clip
joints' and the girls drew commission for soaking the
suckers. They took the stools on either side of him,
expectantly. The barman automatically reached for the
bottle with red coloured liquid, but George stopped him.
'The young ladies will drink the same as me,' he said.
There was a brief pause and glances were exchanged
with the girls. Then he poured three cold beers, which
George took to one of the tables where he could see other
customers coming and going. He discovered his two
companions were really very nice girls and, on learning
that he was English, they plied him with questions about
the King, Buckingham Palace and a multitude of other
things, until George, who had hoped that they would be
the informative ones, couldn't get a word in edgeways. It
was a pleasant half hour, and he left with the girls waving
him off from the doorway.

He walked a short distance to the street corner, where
he was pounced on by a shoe-shine boy. 'Shine, mister?'
he asked, showing a row of gleaming teeth. He was as
black as coal and about 12 years old. George couldn't
resist that smile and climbed into the chair. Whistling all
the time, the 'shoe-shine' buffed his shoes until George
thought the rag would catch fire with the friction, but at
the end, his shoes really shone. He tossed the boy a dollar
and his eyes nearly popped out of his head. 'Gee! Thanks,
mister, you're swell,' he said, doffing his cap.

George saw quite a lot on his first outing, but made the
mistake of asking a policeman which streetcar went to
Central Park. It was then he discovered that half the
American police force was of Irish descent and, as soon as

George's English accent betrayed him, he was again plied with questions about 'the auld country'. It was another hour before he eventually got on the tram. He was a little disappointed in Central Park. He could see that these few acres of green grass would seem like heaven to the masses who lived in this vast overcrowded city, and he knew it wouldn't have been fair to make a comparison to the miles of woods and parkland that formed the Dukeries. He enjoyed the collection of animals that formed a small zoo, but that, too, was nothing compared with Regent's Park Zoo in London. However, it was all new experience and George was all for that, wherever he went.

A few days later, he and the lady's maid set out to see the next item on his list, the Woolworth building, and this at any rate was far from disappointing. It truly was impressive, with its fifty-eight storeys towering into the sky. An express elevator took them to the top with several other tourists, all eager to see the magnificent view over New York. As they stepped from the lift the wind hit them with gale force. A narrow parapet encircled the top pinnacle, with only a waist-high safety rail, and they began to move slowly round, clutching their hats. The view really was breathtaking but as they proceeded further, they became aware that something was amiss and they walked into a nightmare.

A man had climbed out on to the narrow coping and stood with the wind tearing at his clothes and hair, while a few anxious people pleaded with him to return to safety. It made George's blood run cold just to see him poised and swaying between life and certain death. Their guide motioned them not to move in case it should be the spark to send the man over. George took a peep over the edge and felt dizzy at the great height. People in the street below resembled ants scurrying about, and the streetcars looked the size of matchboxes. The lady's maid began to feel faint and George felt unusually impatient. With a man perched out there ready to commit suicide, it was no time to fuss a woman whose corsets were probably too tight. A large policeman began to yell at the man, telling him he was committing an offence, which seemed a silly attitude under the circumstances. At length a priest arrived. George was full of admiration as he climbed out on to the ledge to sit with the man, making signs to tell the policemen to leave it to him, and they talked quietly. Two policemen began to move up on the man's blind side, attempting to take him by surprise and pull him to safety. But at the last moment, he turned and saw them. There was a struggle and he jumped, leaving the policemen holding only his jacket. Sick with horror, they watched him twisting and turning, like a falling leaf, to land spread-eagled on the sidewalk below.

The priest clambered to safety and left after a few words with the policemen. George felt there was no hurry now. The other tourists went down, but he had no desire to join the other 'ants' who converged on the crumpled heap below, so he walked the lady's maid round until she felt better before returning to street level. By this time, the remains had been taken away and it was difficult to believe it had ever happened. The following morning, only the briefest report in the newspaper told how a man released from a mental hospital, after treatment for a nervous disorder, had discovered that his wife had gone off with another man. He had taken his own life by leaping from the top of the Woolworth building. It didn't even give his name.

The family remained in New York, but Sir Frederick's business commitments took him to many other places about America, thus giving George the chance to see other facets of this great country. The miles of prairies, the Grand Canyon and Niagara Falls, where he stood in awe at this miracle of beauty and might, harnessed by the skills of engineering to give power to the nation. A sturdy boat touted for visitors who wished to go under the falls to get a closer look, but George decided that the viewing platform on which he stood was near enough to that roaring deluge of water. He saw places that were only a picture in a book, or a name marked on a map to most people, for travel of this kind was well out of reach for people in his station of life.

When Sir Frederick's business was completed they returned to that teeming metropolis and, before they finally sailed for home, George thought he would try to see a little of the other side of the fence, the side where millionaires did not go. The hotel barman was coloured and, during their conversations, had told George of places that were far removed from the plush luxury a visitor would see on the surface. He hadn't gone into detail, but it was one remark he made that fired George's curiosity. He said New York was a place where the mighty dollar was king and there was no room for the 'bum'. So George set out on his free day to see how the 'bums' lived.

He went looking for the Bronx. A streetcar took him to the edge of town, then he began to walk. Immediately he crossed the boundary he came upon the worst kind of poverty and degradation imaginable. He had seen the poverty of Ireland, and indeed, the back streets of London, but this was appalling – the tall tenements, with overflowing dustbins; filthy streets where starving dogs rummaged amongst the rotting waste strewn in the gutters. Children in dirty rags eyed him suspiciously as he passed, while the adults hung aimlessly out of the top windows, or sat among the flies on the doorsteps. No one spoke, but he could feel their hostility and began to feel uneasy. He was an alien among so many coloured faces and to see another white man coming in the opposite direction was a great relief. As the man approached, he called out to George.

159

'Ah say, fella, do you know where yer bound for?'

George noticed that he was smartly dressed, with a heavy gold chain across his waistcoat, and thought it unlikely that he lived in this neighbourhood.

'I think I'm lost,' George told him and went on to say that he was a visitor to New York and was hoping to see as much as possible before returning to England.

The man smiled. 'Well, you'd better walk back with me, buddy. This is the Bowery and they'd cut your throat here for a dollar.'

On their way back together he told George tales that were enough to curdle his blood. Only weeks previously, a policeman had been caught on his own (normally they patrolled in pairs) and was held upside down, with his head in a drain, until he drowned. The man told him that the most notorious gangsters haunted the area and that it wasn't advisable for strangers to venture there. It occurred to George that for someone who obviously enjoyed a better standard of living his companion was very well informed. Wearing all that gold across his chest in a place like this, why wasn't he robbed? Could it be that he was one of the gangsters he spoke of? George decided not to be too inquisitive. They shook hands amiably before going their separate ways.

While he dressed Sir Frederick for dinner that evening, he mentioned his visit to the seamier side of town and Sir Frederick was horrified.

'Good Lord, George! Whatever made you venture into a place like that?' he said. 'The fellow was right, you were very lucky. You must be careful where you go in future.'

They sailed for home again at the end of October and this time George's padding was more bearable. The weather at sea was rough and windy and only the bravest ventured out on deck. When they docked at Liverpool, his chances of getting through customs without suspicion of

what he had round his waist was aided by a thick overcoat, which hid the bulge as well as keeping out the cold.
Until now, no one had been sure how he had managed to
get the jewellery through. The ladies hadn't asked and,
apart from that one suspicious remark made by the
chauffeur about putting on weight, he had discussed the
matter with no one. Safely back at White Webbs, Duncan
looked at him suspiciously.

'Come on, out with it. I know you've been up to
something, what the hell have you got up your jumper?'

George grinned. 'I've been doing a bit of smuggling,'
he confided, allowing Duncan to see him strip off. As the
padding came away to reveal the jewellery strung round
George's middle, Duncan's eyes lit up with admiration.

'I say, you cunning old bugger!'

Later that same day, he returned the jewellery to the
two ladies. They were full of praise and gratitude and
Lady Orr Lewis handed him a package.

'Well, open it George,' she said. 'If you are meeting
that young lady of yours, you might like to wear it.'

Inside the wrapping was a small box containing a gold
watch and chain. The card with it read:

As a token of our esteem for services rendered.

16

War Breaks Out

In the summer of 1914, the Orr Lewis family went for
their usual holiday in southern France. Despite the
rumours of war, they were determined that nothing
should spoil their annual pleasure. George found this to
be the general attitude of all those who romped on the
sun-drenched beaches of Cannes, Nice and Monaco,
enjoying the sense of false security in their opinion that
Britain still ruled the waves. However, on August 4th,
1914, war was declared and all those who were caught
away from their own country made a dash for home. But
the situation of too many people trying to get aboard too
few boats brought chaos to the French Channel ports.
Enormous sums of money were paid to those with an eye
to the main chance, and anything that would float was
accepted if it could convey the well-to-do English safely

back to their island homes.

Sir Frederick's work with the Admiralty made it of national importance for him to get back at once, but the same priority did not extend to his staff. George was left behind with instructions to get himself, Marshall and the two cars home as best they could. He decided to get the cars to the docks so as to be on the spot when any suitable shipping became available. He packed everything he could, including enough food for several days, into the cars. Since Marshall could only drive one car, he paid a gardener handsomely to drive the other. Confusion was everywhere in France, a conscript country where all able-bodied men rushed to fulfil their obligations and took the horses with them, leaving the streets littered with abandoned carts. Weeping women, with children clinging to their skirts, waved their menfolk off, and shutters were closed over all the shop windows.

A handful of sovereigns secured George a vacant garage on the docks, and they settled down to wait. They made themselves as comfortable as possible, but a few hours later they realised they were without water. There was no water-tap on the quayside and it was evident that they would need a drink quite soon. Locking the cars up, they went out into the streets to find a café. All were closed and shuttered. Having been followed by two French soldiers with fixed bayonets, they found themselves pinned up against a wall, with the points of bayonets sticking in their ribs. George put his hand to his pocket to get the passports, but the move was misconstrued and immediately pressure was applied until George handed over the passports for inspection and gasped the magic words – 'British Consul'. To their relief, the bayonets were lowered and they found themselves embraced in friendship.

Fortunately, George was good at sign language. The gesture of hand to mouth in a drinking motion means only one thing to a Frenchman – wine. The soldiers were all in favour of that and led the way to the side door of a closed café. After explanations to the proprietor, they were welcomed in and several bottles of red wine were produced. The proprietor spoke a little English and George was able to explain their predicament. Immediately two large flagons of distilled water and a dozen bottles of beer were provided and, after more hugs and handshakes, the English party went back laden to the docks to wait.

A week went by. George began to feel desperate. Their food had run out and they needed baths. Many others who were stranded had also gathered on the quay. When a fishing boat arrived, it was everyone for himself. The skipper took those who could pay the most. George parted with £50, all the money he had left, to get his party and the two cars on board. They were packed in like sardines, but they were on their way home at last.

The boat put in at Gravesend. Now they were faced with the problem of getting home to White Webbs without money and without their second driver, who stayed behind in France. They found a post office, where George explained their predicament and got through on the phone to Sir Frederick, who was overjoyed to hear of their safe return. He arranged for the postmistress to lend George £20, for which he signed on Sir Frederick's behalf. Then they put one car into a lock-up garage and set out for Enfield in the other.

On arrival, George found waiting a letter from his brother Arthur saying he intended to join up. George felt this to be premature, considering that most people were of the opinion the war would be over by Christmas. He was as patriotic as the next fellow, but it didn't make sense to abandon one's career for so short a period. He sent a telegram to ask his brother to wait until they could talk it over; then he asked Sir Frederick's opinion, because if Arthur went to war, then he would go with him.

Sir Frederick was adamant. 'You are quite right George,' he said. 'Your brother is already doing a valuable job on the home front, and so are you. The regular army can handle things. That's what it's trained for, and it will all be finished soon, you'll see.'

On his next visit home, he managed to persuade Arthur to wait six months before joining up and made a pact that, if the war wasn't over by then, they would take the King's shilling together. But in the next few weeks it was evident that, despite Sir Frederick's predictions, the end was not in sight, far from it. Hostilities had escalated at sea as well as on the battle fields. A terrible new weapon had been introduced to warfare, the submarine. Ships carrying troops and other essentials were being sunk daily by these silent killers, and there seemed to be very little defence against them.

Sir Frederick's work with the Admiralty was even more important now and it was in this capacity that it became necessary for him to go to Canada. Luxury liners were still keeping their schedule, for nobody feared attacks on them. It was taken for granted that no major power with any decency at all would sink a passenger ship; it simply wasn't done. George packed only bare necessities, and they left without any elaborate preparations. Their passage was as pleasant as any they had made. There was the same holiday atmosphere, with dancing and all the other facilities on board, and there was no shortage of food. It was difficult to believe there was a war on. The voyage passed without incident, except for sighting icebergs off the coast of Newfoundland, and this was significant because, two years previously, they had escaped possible death on the *Titanic* when the vessel struck an iceberg on her maiden voyage. Sir Frederick had been booked to sail on her to a business conference that was cancelled at the last minute. These enormous chunks of ice glinted in the sun, and it was easy to see how the bottom could be ripped out of a ship, especially as eight-ninths more lay under the water than could be seen above it.

They stayed at the Château Frontenac in Quebec for the time it took to complete the business, then sailed home again. Apart from the odd merchant ship in the distance, nothing remotely warlike had been seen in either direction.

Meanwhile, everyone at White Webbs had joined the war effort. Lady Orr Lewis was busy with knitting circles, jumble sales and anything else that would raise money for the Red Cross and comforts for the troops. Colonel Sir Henry Bowles, of the adjacent Forty Hall, had formed a contingent of men for guarding the home front. He mustered all those who were too young to join the regular army, and those who were past the age limit, and put them through their paces in the park every Sunday morning. George was amused when Duncan announced that he had been made Captain of this assorted band. He rode about on his father's hunter, smoking the biggest cigar he could find.

George took a few days' leave and went to Babworth for the harvest festival. He joined in the prayers for those on the battle fields and listened to Sir Albert Whitaker reading the lesson, but after the service he detected a certain resentment from many of the neighbours on the estate whose boys were at the front. He saw his mother's face, as one remarked, 'Isn't it time your lads were showing the flag? We've all got to do our bit, you know.'

It occurred to George what a strange creature the human animal was. Mothers who had shared their joys and sorrows over the years were now almost hostile because their sons were in uniform while others were not. Mrs Chapman, the gamekeeper's wife, had two sons in France. They had joined of their own free will when the war had first begun and, until now, the two families had been very close as neighbours, but there was a truculent glint in her eye too, as she greeted George.

'I keep telling your Mam, you'll have to be changing that fine suit for a khaki one soon, or folk will be talking.'

George amiably replied that the war had scarcely begun and that he wanted to give the professionals time to sort things out, before he interfered. But Arthur was tugging at the leash. He was still smarting from an incident that had occurred a few days previously while walking in the street. A young woman had tucked a white feather into his top pocket as he passed. It had been a great blow to his pride.

'I can tell you, George, that's the first time I've come close to hitting a woman,' he said.

Rufford Abbey had asked some of their more valuable staff to delay enlistment, but Arthur wasn't happy about it. He could see that his parents were being persecuted and confided to George, 'It's all very well these people hanging on to our shirt tails, but they don't have to suffer the opinion of folk who don't know the truth.'

17

Sinking of the Lusitania

Before Christmas Sir Frederick confided to George that he had to make another trip to America and urged him not to contemplate enlisting before that was over. It was a matter of some importance and he would need George more than ever to ensure the visit was a success.

'You are my right-hand man, George,' he said. 'I can't go into details, but I assure you that by accompanying me on this voyage you will be serving your country well.'

They were to sail for New York on March 20th on the *Lusitania*, the fastest vessel afloat and reputed to be unsinkable. Lady Allen and her two daughters were in America at the time that George and Sir Frederick embarked, and it was arranged that they should travel back with Sir Frederick at the beginning of May.

The German High Command at this time was threatening to turn its submarine force against any ship flying the British flag and this caused some apprehension. Sir Frederick brushed it aside as nothing more than rumour.

'Don't listen to the scare-mongers, George,' he said. 'What gain could come from sinking a passenger ship? Even the Germans have their code of honour.'

There is no doubt that the Cunard liner *Lusitania* was a magnificent ship. She was launched at Clydebank in 1906 as a sister ship to the *Mauretania*, truly a floating palace in every sense of the word. The two great liners vied with each other for the 'Blue Riband' trophy for the fastest crossing between Liverpool and New York. A maximum speed in ideal conditions of over 25 knots enabled the *Lusitania* to reduce the passage to under five days. That was rarely achieved in wartime, if for no other reason than the fact – little-known at the time – that the *Lusitania* was run on reduced power to economise on operating costs. Furthermore, both ships were initially financed by the Admiralty in an attempt by the British Government to safeguard its maritime routes in the face of competition from German passenger vessels that were being designed from the outset for easy conversion to warships. The precise role of the *Lusitania* in 1915 has been the subject of much speculation and it can hardly be wondered that the enemy kept a close watch on her.

As Sir Frederick and George went aboard in early spring sunshine, everyone was in high spirits and determined to enjoy the voyage despite the war. Many were the light-hearted remarks heard on that occasion.

'If we meet a submarine, let's offer the captain some champagne and then he'll go away.'

During the voyage, Staff Captain Anderson proudly conducted tours of the engine rooms and other parts of the ship where passengers normally didn't go. George was duly impressed by the massive machinery that drove the great ship. Many who had been nervous about the hostile rumours felt reassured after having the watertight compartments pointed out to them. Little was seen of the *Lusitania*'s new master, Captain Turner, a very experienced seaman who seemed to give all his attention to the business of navigating on the bridge throughout his first voyage aboard the liner.

They docked in New York on schedule and without incident. The United States at that time was not at war, but there were distinct signs of anxiety among the American people. Opinions varied, but in the main Americans were not in favour of launching their country into a war they considered to be none of their business. And who could blame them for that? But rumours were circulating that reprisals would come from the impounding of the German warship *Vaterland*, which had sailed into American waters.

A few days before Sir Frederick and his party were due to embark for the return voyage, some American newspapers carried an advertisement placed by the Imperial German Embassy in Washington, warning that if the *Lusitania* sailed for England she would be sunk. To be fair, it did not name the *Lusitania* specifically, but no one could mistake the timing for anything other than a hint that a trap was being prepared if the great liner undertook the imminent trip home. Many intending passengers took heed and cancelled their passages at the last moment. Again Sir Frederick shrugged it off. He explained to George that a submarine could never match the *Lusitania*'s superior speed and, in any case, the way in which she was built allowed her to stay afloat under any circumstances. All very comforting to hear, but on the day of departure, leaflets repeating the warning were handed out on the quay.

With the extra responsibility of Lady Allen, her two small daughters and her two maids, George didn't have much time to dwell on the dangers. The maids, whose job it was to keep the little Allen girls amused, ran a poor second to George in popularity as a playmate. Two reproachful voices greeted him as he took the air for a few moments at the ship's rail, watching the last of the passengers coming aboard.

'Oh! There you are, George. We've been looking everywhere for you, and we're thirsty.'

As always, George capitulated and was dragged off to find a lemonade. On another such errand once they were at sea, the two little girls tugged George past Lady Allen sunning herself in a deck chair. She smiled to see him caught again.

'It's your own fault, George. You spoil them,' she said.

In the evenings, however, when the two little charmers were in bed, George and the valet he had met during the voyage and the two maids joined in the entertainments on board, especially the dancing.

They had been at sea for a little over five days before passengers began to get edgy with the approach to the coast of Ireland and the waters that had been declared a war zone. In the evening of Thursday May 6th, Sir Frederick went to the concert held in the first-class passengers' smoking room. Even the taciturn Captain Turner, who left most of the socialising to his Staff Captain, bowed to custom and took his seat for the entertainment. In his short speech of thanks at the end, Captain Turner sought to reassure everyone by telling them that he was applying maximum safety measures for their well-being. No one was to be alarmed by the life-boat drill he had called that afternoon, nor by the black-ing out of their cabin windows and portholes. In addition he would be obliged if everyone would refrain from lighting cigars out on deck after dark. He had reduced speed slightly because of the mist and to ensure passing the Fastnet Rock under cover of darkness. By morning they would find a Royal Navy cruiser alongside as escort.

There was always a grand carnival dance on board the night before the ship docked and this trip was no exception. George was up bright and early on the morning of May 7th, to attend to his duties and to start some of the personal packing. He knew there would be no time to see to everything on the following morning, when they were due to dock in Liverpool, and he didn't want to miss any of the last evening's fun and festivities.

He took a turn round E deck before breakfast. The ship's notice-board announced the sighting of the coast of Ireland, but in the fog that had closed in during the early morning no one would be seeing anything. Later in the morning, he watched the children chasing one another round the deck, laughing at their antics. He had arranged to meet his valet friend for a beer at twelve o'clock in one of the bar lounges. George found his friend already at the bar when he arrived. They had scarcely got their beers and settled down to chat when the ship seemed to lurch violently. Someone fell heavily against the bar and several charged glasses crashed to the floor. George and his friend stared at one another momentarily in some consternation before rushing on deck in the confusion to find out what was happening.

The sun was shining now, the mist having almost cleared. No one knew why they had changed course so suddenly. George could now make out the coastline towards which they appeared to be steaming. There was no sign of the cruiser alongside which they had been told to expect. Had some emergency suddenly reached the ears of the Captain on the bridge to cause him hastily to seek the shelter of Queenstown harbour? It had happened before, that the *Lusitania* had put in there on the homeward trip.

As no immediate explanation was forthcoming and

everything appeared to calm down again, George and his friend returned to their drinks in the bar. But so engaged did they become with their conversation that they failed to notice the time passing and missed their places at the one o'clock sitting for luncheon in the dining saloon, where they had agreed to meet the two maids. E deck was almost deserted as they made their way to their rendez-vous. They found the maids waiting for them by a window on the starboard side of the second-class dining saloon towards the stern of the ship. They waved as George and his companion entered. Apologies were made and the steward took their order. It was already past two o'clock. George did not know what made him at that moment gaze out to sea. His eye was caught by a disturbance in the calm water, like a long furrow speckled with white, advancing rapidly in a straight line in the direction of the forepart of the ship. Although he had never seen anything like it before, he knew instantly what it must be. Before he had time to draw the attention of the others to it, the torpedo struck.

The impact was so violent that the great ship seemed to lurch out of the water. Up on the balcony, the orchestra was playing a lively rendering of 'It's a long way to Tipperary' when the explosion occurred, and the grand piano was flung through the balustrading, to land with a discordant crash in the middle of the dining saloon. There was an ear-splitting sound of breaking glass and crockery and a pall of scalding steam billowed in through the doorway. Black smoke and dust descended in a choking cloud and the ship took on a steep list to starboard, making it difficult to stay on one's feet. Seconds later came another loud explosion, presumably a second tor-pedo, and the list worsened, throwing everyone in a heap. They clawed at one another in fear and desperation and George struggled as hard as any. Stark panic was breaking out as they realised their plight and, through this screaming nightmare, George managed to get himself out on deck.

It was now difficult to breathe in the fumes and thick black smoke. People ran screaming the names of loved ones who were missing. George had never seen such panic in his life. He hauled himself along the sloping deck, holding on to anything that would keep him upright. Those able to swim were discarding their shoes and diving overboard. Immediately they touched the water, some were sucked back into the bowels of the ship through a gaping hole in the ship's side on the waterline. The crew were trying to launch the lifeboats, but the angle of the ship made it almost impossible. George saw one boatload of children reach the water safely, only to be sunk by those struggling in the water. They hauled themselves aboard until the boat became overloaded and spilled the lot into the sea.

E deck was one below the dining saloon. Had George been berthed in the first-class cabins at this level towards the bows of the ship, he would have found them already under water. Many of the portholes had been left open on the starboard side and thousands of tons of water cascaded in to the forward cabins of both E and D deck within seconds of the first impact. Though the list to starboard had increased in the minutes it took him to struggle to his own cabin in the rear, he found himself having to scramble up a steep slope as the ship's stern rose out of the water.

Shielding his face from scalding steam, he groped his way along corridors strewn with debris and filled with smoke. He found his cabin door wrenched from its hinges and jammed tight in the doorway. There was no time to be lost. The ship slipped to an even greater list. He struggled to move the door enough to get through, but discovered his life jacket was gone. In panic, people had rushed to the nearest cabins and had taken the first life jacket they could lay hands on; now George was driven to do the same. He went from cabin to cabin, eventually finding three. He struggled into one and, clutching the other two, started back, with the ship groaning ominously under his feet. On the stairs, panic-stricken people tackled him frantically for possession of his life jackets, but George fought just as hard to keep them. He dragged himself up to a higher deck and began to search the screaming throng for Sir Frederick and Lady Allen. He jostled with weeping women, their terrified children clinging to them, all struggling to get to the lifeboats, treading on the injured lying about the decks in their panic to get away.

On the port side, George found a man brandishing a revolver and demanding to know why lifeboats weren't being lowered. A crewman with an axe in his hand said the Captain had ordered that boats weren't to be launched. No one appreciated the catastrophes that had occurred trying to launch boats while the ship was still moving rapidly through the water. Under threat of shooting, the seamen knocked out the pin and the boat, loaded with passengers, crashed down on to others clambering up the sloping deck.

Then George spotted Lady Allen over by the ship's rails, hugging her two children to her. The little girls spotted him and ran with open arms to greet him, their pretty faces full of trust.

'Don't cry, Mamma, it's all right now. George has found us and he will know what to do.'

George couldn't have described his feelings at that moment. Those who scorn the life of a servant in those days could never understand the pride and satisfaction he felt at the little girls' words. They prized and trusted him, even in a terrible situation like this. What more could any other employment have brought?

He hugged them too and Her Ladyship burst into tears.

'Oh! George, how glad we are to see you!' she said. George inquired about Sir Frederick, but she said she hadn't seen him since luncheon, when he had gone to his cabin to take a rest. George knew he wasn't there because he had been to his cabin at the rear of the first-class berths before going in search of life jackets.

They fought their way through the chaos to where another lifeboat was being launched on the other side of the ship. At least they might get the children away. The two maids were there waiting their turn to get into the boat and, during the time it took to strap the little girls into the spare life jackets, he gave them orders to take charge, once they were safely in the boat. Then he noticed that Lady Allen was also without a jacket and, despite her protests, George gave up his own, deciding that he would have to take his chance. This side of the ship listed badly over the water, but it did make launching easier. The lifeboat hung away from the side and it was a shorter distance down to the water. He fought with other terrified passengers to get the children into the boat and the crew lifted the two maids in as the boat was lowered. There wasn't room for Lady Allen and, smiling bravely for the children's benefit, she waved them off with tears in her eyes. The boat reached the water safely, swirled for a moment, like a leaf caught on the tide then, with strong strokes, the oarsmen pulled clear of the suction area and struck out for the distant shore.

The sea was now a mass of struggling people and it was dreadful to see how they scrambled for the smallest piece of wreckage. They managed to launch another boat, but as it touched the water, it was immediately capsized by a number of people who jumped from the decks in the hope of getting into it at the last moment. The ship suddenly lurched again and the list worsened. People were thrown off their feet and rolled, like ninepins, down the deck and over the edge. George clung desperately to some rigging. After this, no more boats could be launched because of the angle of the ship. Those who were left on board now had only one chance of survival – the fervent hope that rescue would be in time.

It was just thirty-six miles from Queenstown, and about eleven from the Head of Kinsale – near enough to have seen land, if it were not for the thick pall of black smoke. Surely the message about their distress must have reached the coast guards at least? The ship lurched again and slid further down into the water. People began to climb up the steep slope towards the stern as the *Lusitania* rolled almost on to her side. George followed their example, holding grimly to the rails and trying to keep with Lady Allen, but in the mad scramble he lost sight of her. If the ship rolled over, George debated, perhaps he could run on to her side. A crazy thought, but he was ready to try anything rather than share his brother John's fate. He thought back to that terrible day, when he had walked with that stretcher carrying his brother's lifeless body. He remembered his grief-stricken mother and he prayed for something – anything – that would spare his mother from such anguish again. At that moment, he lost his grip and rolled down the steep slope, quite expecting to end up in the sea. Instead he rolled against one of the huge funnels and made a grab at the rigging. He noticed that Captain Turner was only a few yards away clinging on to one of the ventilators. True to the code, he had stayed with his ship.

As if in answer to his prayer, the great ship suddenly gave a loud groan and, although it was very low in the water, she levelled out on a more even keel. Hopefully he scanned the horizon for any sign of rescue, but in vain. George prayed that some of those watertight compartments would stay watertight. There was a terrible rumbling sound coming from the interior, followed by another violent lurch and the water was now washing over his feet. Then came a blinding explosion from the boilers below, which blew off one of the funnels in a cloud of scalding steam, and he felt himself lifted off his feet. He was air-borne and, he remembered thinking briefly, at least going in the right direction. Seconds later he was dumped into the sea.

George was drawn down into a whirl-pool of green bubbles and wreckage. His lungs were bursting and his eyes felt as though they were being gouged out of their sockets. He tried to prepare himself for death, but another great explosion occurred and he felt himself rushing upwards at great speed. He shot up, like a cork, and was flung high into the air before finally being dumped back into the sea clear of the suction area. His limbs felt like leaden weights, numbed by the icy water, but his mind stayed alert. A large piece of wreckage floated within reach and he grabbed it and clung on. It seemed to be a door from one of the cabins and it kept his head above water until he could summon enough strength to hoist himself on to it. He lay dazed, his eyes painful and swollen. He felt weak and fought to remain conscious. There was no feeling in his legs and each breath was agony. Men, women and children were being washed against one another by the turbulence where the ship was rapidly plunging beneath the water. Some floated face down, their limbs loose and lifeless, while others clawed over them to keep themselves afloat. The screaming had ceased now, but the low moans of the dying was something George remembered all his life.

Suddenly his raft began to pitch and toss violently, as another drowning soul made a bid for life. George was powerless to help him, but eventually the man struggled on and lay gasping for breath. As the smoke and steam cleared, he could see that the *Lusitania* had groaned her last. She was gone.

All hope was fading now. There was still no sign of rescue from any direction and yet they were so near to the coast of Ireland. Surely, the sinking of that great ship could not have gone unnoticed. At least one of the life-boats must have reached the shore by now. Water began to wash over George's face as he realised that the raft had been invaded to the extent that it had sunk beneath the water. The next minute he was tipped into the sea. For a time, he kept himself afloat by holding on to the dead and dying, until a cylinder floated near. He made a frantic effort to catch it, but it was very bouyant and bounced about in the water. With an effort born out of sheer desperation, he managed to grasp one end and held on grimly.

It would be difficult to describe the intense coldness of the sea as an eerie stillness descended on that dreadful scene, for those who still grappled with a spark of life were too weak to cry out. A stewardess managed to get a grip on the other end of George's cylinder and, for a while, this helped a lot, because it kept it more stable in the water, with one on either end. She was covered in thick black oil and began to make awful gurgling noises in her throat. George tried to speak to her, but his tongue was too swollen and his efforts were ignored anyway. She clung for a while and then slid down in the water. In the struggle to retain his hold on the cylinder, which bounced violently, he lost sight of her. He found the only way to keep a tight hold on it now was to embrace it.

Time began to lose all meaning. He was so numb that his mind drifted between consciousness and oblivion. He tried to think of those at home, but his thoughts became jumbled with frightening things, groups of men, dancing frenziedly, with grotesque faces. In his delirium, he saw his own funeral, with flowers heaped on the coffin, and his family gathered at Babworth churchyard. A little girl washed against him, bringing back reality for a moment.

He remembered seeing her running round the deck, with her fair ringlets flying out behind. She was quite still, her eyes closed, as the current carried her away. The sun was gone now and a stiff wind was increasing the water's turbulence. He was finding it difficult to breathe and he couldn't think any more – he didn't want to. It was much easier just to go to sleep and George allowed himself to drift into a long dark tunnel and merciful peace.

∾ 18 ∾
Survivor in Queenstown

A flicker of life returned to George with a voice that said, 'I t'ink there's one over here wid a bit o'loife in him.'

George was aware of being pummelled and felt resentful at being disturbed. Something that burnt was being poured down his throat, making him splutter and flashing lights danced before his eyes. As the clouds of unconsciousness parted, he tried to remember, something – anything – but it hurt. Suddenly, he could smell something familiar, but he couldn't think what it was. Then came that voice again, and more pummelling.

'Come on now, me foine boy'o – come on wid ye now.'

More fiery liquid was being poured down his throat and, as he choked his heart up, his memory came flooding back. He tried to move, but a restraining arm held him and the voice out of the darkness came again.

'That's better, come on now, you have some o'this, it'll set ye up foine.'

His memory was returning with a rush, of screaming people, his boss, Lady Allen and those two little girls. He became aware that he was wrapped in a blanket and that the 'voice' was bending over him. He suddenly knew that accent – it was Irish. The familiar smell was tar from fishing nets. His mind briefly recalled his last visit to Ireland, when he had chatted with the fishermen and marvelled at the nimbleness of their fingers as they mended the tools of their trade. Through cracked lips, he asked where he was and was told that he was safely on board a torpedo boat. The mere mention of the word 'torpedo' was enough to bring the dreadful events following the death of the *Lusitania* back to him. He asked to be allowed to sit up. Painfully he was propped against the wall, where he could see something of his surroundings. The cabin was small and, by the light of the lantern that hung from the ceiling, he was horrified to see that the deck was piled high with bodies. The seaman was speaking again.

'By all that's holy, ye had the saints on your side this night. Fished ye out like a mackerel – so we did.'

The life coming back to George's limbs was almost unbearable. He asked the time, and was told that it was ten o'clock in the evening. He had survived those terrible conditions for seven and a half hours. Suddenly he began to vomit and, with the seaman supporting him, he got rid of large quantities of the Atlantic ocean from his stomach. He learned later that they had cleared his lungs by artificial respiration, but now he felt that he would die all over again. With tears of weakness wetting his face, they made him comfortable in a sitting position and left him to recover a little. Then they gave him small sips of hot soup before he fell into a sleep of exhaustion.

It was daylight when he awoke and, although he felt as if he had been put through a mangle, he was refreshed and able to sit up by his own efforts. His rescuer brought him some more hot soup, which he drank gratefully. The piles of bodies were still there, a pitiful sight to behold, and George whispered a prayer for them and for his own miraculous escape. He asked the seaman to help him to stand up and, after a wobbly start, he was able to totter as far as the ablution. Here he was able to take a look at himself in a small mirror and he could hardly believe that the face looking back at him was his own. It was the face of an old man, not one of only twenty-six. It was bloated and blistered by the long soaking in icy sea water, and his eyes were swollen slits. His lips were cracked and bleeding and great hollows were where his once healthy cheeks had been. He was also aware of a searing pain in his right foot and lowered himself down into a sitting position. He saw that his foot was swollen to twice the normal size and one trouser leg was missing.

They put in to Queenstown harbour, where George was helped ashore to the waiting cameras and newsmen. As they began to unload the bodies, an old priest took George into his care. They travelled by donkey-cart to a crude building some distance from the harbour, where they were received by the nuns, who were giving what assistance they could to a number of other survivors in a similar condition. They bound his injured foot, and provided him with some warm clothing. In normal times, it would have been a big laugh to see the usually so immaculate George in such a strange assortment of garments. There was an overcoat that had seen the best of its days and was about four sizes too large for him, a pair of corduroy trousers and a hefty pair of hob-nailed boots, which he was unable to wear because of his injured foot. The boots were exchanged for a pair of white plimsolls without laces. The sisters were marvellous, and gave what little they had to those who had survived the cruel sea. George slept on the wooden floor that night, and relished the hot vegetable stew they provided, but the following morning he explained that he had to go in search of Sir Frederick and the others in his party and, reluctantly, they let him go.

Painfully, he hobbled into Queenstown. He had no money, for all his possessions had gone down with the ship, except a few items that had been on his person. All his clothes, his passport and even his precious tie-pin, which had been a present from Lady Allen, were now at the bottom of the sea. Only his gold watch was left in his pocket, with the hands now stationary, marking the time of 2.30 p.m., a grim reminder of being flung into the icy sea, and of all that followed on that terrible May 7th, 1915.

George began his search at the police station, but they were unable to help him. The survivors had been scattered wherever they could be accommodated and there hadn't been time to make an inventory. He was advised to go down to the harbour, where they were still bringing bodies in by the boat load. Sharks had invaded the area and many of the victims, who had been skimmed up in the fishing nets, were mutilated beyond recognition. It was a sickening sight, as George picked his way through that macabre scene to the harbour master's office. He got no information here either. Everywhere he inquired he got the same answer, and in the end he was going from door to door in his search.

After several wearisome hours, his patience was rewarded, for he found Sir Frederick in a cheap lodging house not far from the water-front. The place was filthy and was obviously a haunt for lonely sailors who needed a bed, with possibly female company provided as well.

Being so near to the harbour, it was also infested with rats. There George found Sir Frederick in a pitiful state. He lay on a straw mattress on the floor of a small top room, looking like death, but they were both overjoyed to be reunited.

George discovered two five pound notes in Sir Frederick's pocket. They were saturated with sea water, but he was able to restore them well enough to be acceptable and, with these, he went to find a doctor. This was no easy task, for there were very few doctors in Queenstown and they were rushed off their feet with the influx of patients. The first surgery he called at was packed and a very harassed receptionist told him he would just have to wait his turn. He went on to the next, determined this time not to take 'No' for an answer. He pushed his way through the waiting room and into the surgery, where he pleaded almost hysterically that if Sir Frederick didn't receive some attention soon he would die. The doctor must have noticed that George was near to collapse himself, and packed his bag right away, leaving the nurse in charge.

They found Sir Frederick in a state of semi-consciousness and, while the doctor got to work, George hobbled off to find more suitable accommodation. The only hotel in Queenstown was full – or so they said until George produced one of the five pound notes. Then suddenly a small top room that was vacant was remembered. It was far short of the Ritz Carlton, but infinitely better than the hovel Sir Frederick was in at the moment, so he paid in advance and returned to find that, although very weak, Sir Frederick was now fully conscious. The doctor had left instructions that he was to be kept warm for a few days and to be given light nourishing meals. George approached the landlady about this, only to be told sharply, 'I only do bed and breakfast. I can't do special meals for anyone.'

The hotel was not too far away and George decided it would be better to get Sir Frederick there as soon as possible. He was still very weak and was in only his under-vest. George asked what had happened to his shirt, and Sir Frederick told him how a young man had brought him to this place and had offered to get his shirt laundered, but hadn't returned. George instantly knew why. It hadn't all been out of kindness that this service had been offered; he had probably noticed the cuff-links that George had put into the sleeves on the morning of the disaster. They had been a birthday present to Sir Frederick from Her Ladyship, and had originally been especially made for King Edward VII. They were an exclusive design of diamonds and emeralds in a fine gold setting, but the King hadn't liked them and had returned them to the jeweller for re-sale. They were worth in the region of a thousand pounds. George was rather doubtful that they would see either the shirt or the young man again.

Painfully, they set out and shivered their way through the streets in the bitter wind blowing in from the sea. Sir Frederick had to be supported every inch of the way, and the strain on George's injured foot was agony. But at last he was able to get Sir Frederick to bed with a hot-water bottle, where immediately he fell asleep. George needed rest badly himself, but there was still much to be done. As tired as he was, a driving influence made him determined to get some order back into this terrible situation and to find some warm clothing. He went to a pawnbroker, where he bought a black suit, turning green in places, for Sir Frederick and a pair of worsted trousers for himself. Then, with his purchases done up in a brown paper parcel, he made for the post office, where he sent off two telegrams, one to White Webbs and the other to Babworth, before hobbling back to the hotel.

Sir Frederick was still sleeping, so George bathed his foot in cold water and tightened the bandage to try to stop the swelling. It was extremely painful and, after all the tramping about he had done, he felt he had to rest awhile. With Sir Frederick occupying the only bed, he made do with two chairs pushed together and his overcoat for warmth.

The following morning he was stiff and sore. His foot had swollen to the size of a large pudding basin and the pain made him feel faint. Only great determination got him down to breakfast, for there was no room service. He was allowed to take scrambled egg to Sir Frederick before sitting down to kippers with the other guests.

It was now May 10th, three days after the disaster, and still no help had come from the Government, or indeed any other department. It was almost as though they had been abandoned and were now an embarrassment. In spite of the dense plume of smoke and all the other evidence of the great ship's distress, which couldn't have gone unnoticed so near to land, rescue had been left far too late and, even now, nobody seemed to care a damn for those who, by the grace of God, had survived.

Lady Allen, her two young daughters and the maids were still missing. After breakfast, George went again to the police station, where a list of sorts had been posted. There were a few names of those like himself who had come to make inquiries and he added his own name and Sir Frederick's before he left. The constable told him that the harbour was being used as a mortuary because there wasn't any other place large enough to accommodate the fourteen hundred men, women and children who had perished. The harbour had been screened off with canvas, leaving only a gap for people to walk round in single file. George joined the waiting queue and watched the faces of those who came out. It was clear whether the loved ones had been found, by the stricken expressions on their faces, but he could never have imagined what lay behind those canvas screens.

Eventually George's turn came and, dreading the ordeal, he went in and shuffled his way between the rows of bodies, laid out like a fishmonger's slab. They were all just as they had been dragged from the sea and it horrified him to look upon the remnants of what had once been human life. Bloated with sea water, their faces twisted and grotesque, they were covered in green slime and thick black engine oil, many with limbs missing, where the sharks had got there before the fishing boats. There was a young nurse-maid, clutching twin babies, one in either arm. Even in death, she had not relinquished her duty to her two tiny charges. There were rows of children of all ages, and here he stopped in his tracks, for among them were the two dear little Allen girls who, so short a time ago, had begged him to 'come and play'. They were bloated and mottled and still wearing the life jackets he himself had put on them. Somehow he forced himself to continue, for Lady Allen and the two maids were yet to be found. The lump in his throat threatened to choke him. Then, with tears streaming down his face, he blundered out of that gruesome place, to walk the streets for a long time. The pain in his injured foot was nothing to the pain in his heart. He had to regain his composure before taking the sad news back to Sir Frederick.

Fortunately, Sir Frederick was much improved. The doctor had called again and had allowed him to get up for a few hours. He took the sad news much more calmly than George had anticipated, and showed great concern for Lady Allen. George hobbled off again, this time to the place where he really should have gone in the beginning, the small cottage hospital. However, George's usual common sense was not at its best, his head felt as though it were filled with cotton wool, as he staggered into reception and, before he could state his business, collapsed in a heap on the floor. George had never fainted in his life before, but it did serve to get him the attention he so badly needed. He came round to find himself in a small ward with the doctor in attendance. An examination showed that his instep was broken and, for the first time since the shipwreck, it was properly treated. On inquiry, he learned that Lady Allen and her two maids had been admitted suffering from exposure, but were now recovering satisfactorily. He told the doctor that he was the bearer of sad news for Her Ladyship and, to George's great relief, the doctor volunteered to break the news for him. Although the small hospital was filled to capacity, they wanted to ward George, but he explained that he had his duties to Sir Frederick, who was also a sick man, and so they were content to strap his foot securely, give him a crutch and let him go.

❧ 19 ❧
Local Hero

By the end of that terrible week news of the *Lusitania* disaster had shocked the free world. The fact that there had been a great many important Americans aboard made it America's business too. Germany was justly condemned for its crime against humanity and, to the present day, despite German denials of an illegal sinking, the destruction of the *Lusitania* is a blot on Germany's name.

In all 1,201 lives were lost, yet the event was marked by joyful acclaim in the German Press and schoolchildren were given an extra holiday. A special medal was struck in commemoration, one of which came into George's hands after the war and was kept among his many mementoes. It bears on one side an engraving of the ship going down and on the reverse the figure of a skeleton

Local Hero

giving out tickets at the booking office. The legend 'No Contraband' appears above the sinking ship. But it seems less likely that George had acquired a grisly celebration, or indeed justification, on the part of the German Government than one of the souvenirs which were manufactured by the owner of a leading London department store and circulated throughout the world by British Naval Intelligence to bring Germany into even worse odour for its heinous deed.

Germany answered the accusers by claiming that the *Lusitania* not only carried munitions and contraband, but that the ship had been used as a troop-carrier. As an armed vessel, flying a United States flag of convenience yet under the direct command of the Royal Navy, it was therefore claimed as a prize of war. Whatever evidence German intelligence had acquired – and three Germans with a camera were actually found on board in New York and locked up for the duration of that fateful voyage – the premeditated and unprovoked torpedo attack on the *Lusitania* was certainly an act of homicide against a large number of innocent civilians, many of them citizens of a neutral power.

Many attempts have been made by salvage divers, one as recently as 1983, to ascertain whether the *Lusitania* was indeed carrying an illicit cargo of gold bullion. The ship lies in only some 300 feet of water, less than 12 miles off the southern coast of Ireland, yet there are enormous difficulties in getting into her (as Colin Simpson amply illustrates in the Epilogue he added to the latest Penguin edition of his excellent book *Lusitania*). Official documents suggest that it was unlikely. No such doubts can remain, however, that the ship was carrying a considerable concealed and improperly documented cargo of dangerous and warlike materials, including bars of copper, a large consignment of brass rods, several thousand cases of shrapnel shells and live rifle ammunition, and a quantity of fuel oil – all packed into cargo holds in the bows, specially constructed when it appeared in 1913 that war might be imminent. Most of this contraband was effectively hidden by barrels of oysters and by a consignment of dairy produce destined for delivery to the Co-operative Wholesale Society. Nothing short of a full inspection of the *Lusitania* wreck can confirm one way or the other whether the ship had been armed with her own concealed guns in that hushed-up pre-war refit.

Among others, Colin Simpson continues to speculate about the Admiralty's motives in withdrawing the cruiser escort that was scheduled to conduct the *Lusitania* safely through the Irish Sea to her docking at Liverpool. U-boats had already sunk a number of vessels off the southern coast of Ireland. Winston Churchill, at the time First Lord of the Admiralty, has even been accused of employing devious means whereby to exercise his grand strategy of implicating neutral states (in particular the United States) in the war against Germany, and the loss of American life in the *Lusitania* disaster certainly enraged the American government. It can hardly be credited that so many innocent lives would have been sacrificed in such a cause, yet the evidence is there to suggest that less than the whole blame can be laid on the Germans.

Whatever the truth of the matter, little was done to help the 746 survivors. While the feuding countries threw accusations back and forth, the victims were burying their dead in the Old Church Cemetery. George stood with a great crowd to pay his last respects and watched the processions of coffins go by. On that day he recalled the words of the old Irish lace-maker who, years before, had looked into her teacup and forecast the tragic circumstances under which he would next set foot on Irish soil.

Before long Sir Frederick had recovered sufficiently to be able to return home. The survivors had been given facilities to telegraph news of their safety to their loved ones. George sent a telegram to Dorothy to say that he was on his way home. It was an all too brief message, but enough to send the Lawrence family wild with joy. A party was planned by George's friends at the Rose and Crown, where they looked forward to carrying the returning hero shoulder high into the midst of the celebrations. Lady Allen had already returned home, full of praise for George's attempt to save her two daughters and for giving up his own life jacket to her, knowing that he was unable to swim. She was in no doubt that she owed her life to him.

There was similar rejoicing at Babworth, even the Whitakers joining in. They produced a bottle of champagne at his cottage home, and it became a family joke that George's mother, who had never tasted champagne before, grudgingly admitted that it wasn't bad sort of stuff, even if, in her opinion, it couldn't hold a candle to her elderberry wine. Brother Arthur too did his share of celebrating, in the company of old friends from Rufford and Welbeck, and had to be taken home over the back of a pony.

Meanwhile, Sir Frederick and George had had to wait their turn for places on the overcrowded boats back to England, eventually obtaining passage on a cattle boat. George was fearful about going to sea again after his terrible ordeal, but there was no alternative. On their day of departure, it poured torrents of rain. As they stood on the jetty, George's stomach was a battery of nerves. The cattle were loaded first. As the bedraggled passengers followed them on board, the sickening stench coming up from the hold did little to alleviate their apprehensions. Normally such vessels did not accommodate passengers and so few facilities were

available for their comfort. They sat out on deck in the
rain and stared disconsolately at a turbulent sea. It
caused some amusement among members of the crew
to see George wearing a hastily-acquired life jacket
throughout the relatively short crossing of the Irish sea,
but he didn't care a damn what anyone thought: he had
been caught once and was determined it should never
happen again.

Marshall was waiting with the car when they docked.
He had brought plenty of warm rugs and a bottle of
whisky to ensure their comfort on the journey to White
Webbs. He looked curiously at George, who was still
wearing his white plimsolls, but like a tactful servant
kept his curiosity in check.

When they reached White Webbs a phalanx of jour-
nalists and cameramen chased them up the drive to the
house. It was the first George knew of his acclaim as the
local hero and it was a bit unnerving to find himself in
the limelight. Lady Orr Lewis had done her best to get
rid of the newsmen before the pair of survivors arrived,
but they were not to be denied the full story.

'You'd better see them, George,' she said. 'They
won't go away until you do.'

Unshaven and wearing the clothes the nuns had provided, George quietly answered all their questions in the
drawing room at White Webbs. He explained that there
hadn't been much time to consider the sense or folly of
his actions that day. After all, from the first impact of
the torpedo, it had taken less than twenty minutes for
the whole of that mighty ship to disappear beneath the
waves. As to the life jacket, it had merely been a case of
priorities: Lady Allen had been without one and he had
been able to provide her with one. Any man worth his
salt would have done the same. He suggested that if they
wanted a hero, they should go to the trenches where
heroes were being made every day.

All this reticence seemed only to add to George's popularity. Seeing his unkempt appearance in the newspaper photographs, he thought he looked more like an escaped convict than a local hero. All he really wanted was to try to erase the mental picture of that tiny harbour, with all those dead faces. Instead, people stopped him in the street to shake his hand.

Then came the red tape and rigmarole of form-filling that always goes with claiming compensation. George attended a panel of doctors, who agreed unanimously that his instep had been broken in such a way as to cause a permanent disability; indeed it had already begun to knit into a very ugly lump across the front of his foot. His inventory of lost possessions and their estimated value was whittled down. In the end he received an award of £100. Not a substantial sum, even in 1915, but he consoled himself with the thought that at least he was alive.

The saga of the *Lusitania* dragged on. People were asking how it could have been allowed to happen at all. Those in high places were hard put to provide an answer. It might have saved a lot of political embarrassment if Captain Turner, master of the *Lusitania*, had perished with his ship, for then he could have been the scapegoat the authorities were looking for. But Captain Turner had survived and was fighting for his reputation. It was suggested that he had departed from his scheduled course. His reduced speed and the timing of his approach to the St George's Channel were also questioned.

At the Court of Inquiry, held in mid-June in the Central Hall, Westminster, twenty surviving members of the crew were called as witnesses and only five of the 135 passengers who had written reports. American affidavits were ignored, but a further six members of the public provided evidence. None of the passengers called referred to an explosion at the forward end of the ship.

George never learned what became of his account. The Captain of the U.20 had maintained he fired only one torpedo, yet a second explosion had rocked the stricken *Lusitania*. Was the speed with which the liner nose-dived to the bottom due to the cargo of munitions exploding in the bow holds? Could it be that Sir Frederick, with his Admiralty connections and secret assignments, knew more than he ever owned up to George?

Few thought the inquiry as it was summed up by Lord Mersey totally impartial, though Captain Turner was exonerated from all blame. George was irritated by the complacent tone of the findings published on July 17th, which brought the whole painful episode back to him, like sucking on an aching tooth.

It was not until some time after the Court of Inquiry completed its deliberations that George was able to go home to Babworth. Needless to say, the family gave him a joyful welcome. He was relieved to find that the resentment shown by some of the neighbours on his last visit had been swept away by events, though his brother Arthur was still suspected of dodging the column. Practically every able-bodied young male on the estate was now in uniform. 'Young Master Jackie' Whitaker had gone to France with his regiment, leaving Arthur feeling like the tail on the donkey. The war that people had said would be over by Christmas was fast approaching its second Christmas as it still raged on in ever-worsening conditions for both men and animals. To add to the misery of existing like rats in mud-filled trenches, often ill-fed and ill-clad, the troops were now also at the mercy of Germany's latest weapon – chlorine gas. As yet, the horrors of mustard gas were still unimagined. George had already experienced enough of the enemy's mercy in war. He had only to close his eyes to see again the rows of dead faces in that small Queenstown harbour. Yet the brothers felt impelled to make their contribution to the defeat of people who brought such horrors into the world.

It was easier to make the resolve, however, than to carry it out. Both their employers were desperate at the prospect of losing such vital members of their almost irreplaceable staff. Though Sir Frederick understood George's feelings after all they had been through together, he still maintained that George was doing vital war work already by working for him. Neither George nor Arthur wished to leave their respected benefactors high and dry at the start of a very busy season, but both were adamant that they would join up together as soon as they could reasonably be spared from present employment. Their parents took the news calmly and, with reluctant resignation, so did Sir Frederick.

George and Arthur desperately wanted to remain together in the army. Had they been able to volunteer together before Christmas 1915 it might have been possible. With the passing of the Military Services Act early in 1916, George was to find that he could no longer enlist where he liked. Instead of the two signing on together in their home town, George found that, owing to his long residence in Enfield, he would be registered in North London. The best that could be arranged was to enlist on the same day and apply for the same regiment.

At Mill Hill, George was received by the recruiting sergeant, given an identity card and sent before a medical board. Apprehensively he entered a large waiting room, where a number of men sat around naked, looking pensive. He was told to strip off in one of the cubicles and take his turn with the rest. It came as a shock to a fellow who had always enjoyed his privacy. He was determined to keep his trousers until the very last minute, which caused some ribald jokes on the part of the others waiting. Then someone caused a stir by confiding that he had no intention of joining what he called 'their bloody fiasco'. He had a friend, he told them, who worked in a hospital and who had given him an infallible way of working his ticket.

'I've got a decent job and responsibilities at home,' he said. 'They're not getting me to fight their bloody war, not if I can help it.'

They watched him chew his way through half a bar of Sunlight soap which, he explained, produced every symptom of heart disease. He could scarcely have realised he was one of the first conscripts among a gathering largely made up of eager volunteers.

The examination began and they were called in turn to see the doctors. George noticed the soap-eater had suddenly gone very quiet and was looking decidedly under the weather. His countenance changed from a flushed pink to deathly white, and finally to a grey-green, before he was finally sick. A doctor came to attend to him and the game was up, for there were enough soap suds on the floor to have done the weekly wash. He was taken into the consulting room at once and emerged after a short time with a strained expression and clutching a card which read 'A.1'.

When George's turn came, he was first handed a list of disorders and told to tick those with which he had been afflicted at any time. George hadn't realised there were so many ailments. When the physical examination began, the ugly lump on his instep was noticed almost at once. He had decided not to mention his recent experience as a passenger on the ill-fated *Lusitania*, in case it jeopardised his chances of being accepted; now he was obliged to explain. He answered all their questions and pleaded to be allowed to enter the army, but the examiners were adamant: he would be of no use to the armed forces with an injury of that kind. They graded him C.3, with a recommendation for other work of national importance.

The only person to be pleased by this outcome was Sir Frederick, who considered that George was already engaged in work of national importance, by working for him in his present position. He was convinced that he could get George exempt from what he called 'mundane labour'.

'It would be such a damned silly waste, George,' he said. 'In the time they take to teach you how to operate the machinery, the war will be over and I shall have lost a good valet needlessly.'

George was inclined to agree with him in one respect; nobody could have rated him highly as a handyman. He knew his own profession, but he had never been able to knock a nail in straight. At the moment he was too disappointed to care.

He wrote to his brother, telling him the news. Several days later Arthur replied that he had been accepted for the army. Their plan to be together was not to be fulfilled, and Arthur was sent to France almost immediately after his call-up in the spring of 1916.

With backing from Colonel Sir Henry Bowles, Sir Frederick set the wheels in motion to get George deferred on medical grounds. Once again George had to present himself to a board of doctors. They discovered that, as well as the injury to the foot, he also had a heart murmur, mainly due to damage to his nervous system. They said this would rectify naturally in time, and they deferred his call-up for a minimum of six months, after which they would examine him again.

At least this gave Sir Frederick time to complete another business voyage to America. When George learned that he would be required to accompany him, his courage almost failed him. Sir Frederick confided that he too felt apprehensive at crossing the Atlantic again so soon, but pointed out that this was war work for George. They crossed in the Dutch ship *Rotterdam*, steaming over almost the exact spot where the *Lusitania* had gone down. A short service was conducted on deck and a wreath was floated in memoriam. George slept only fitfully during the whole voyage and was haunted by those two pretty young faces of the little girls who had vied for his favour.

They stayed a week in New York, where it was now apparent that the sinking of the *Lusitania* was like a keg of gunpowder; all it needed was a spark. There was even talk that in the end Americans would have to 'go in and finish the job' – which rather irritated the patriotic George at the time. It was such a provoking statement, when Great Britain and the Empire, Belgium, France and umpteen other countries had been up to their necks in mud and blood for the past two years. In the event, it was left until April 1917 before the United States entered into open hostilities against Germany.

With Sir Frederick's business over, they returned to England without incident. On a visit to the Lawrences' home, George found all the girls stitching for all they were worth. Pretty Connie had said 'Yes' to her soldier sweetheart and they were to be married on his embarkation leave. There was little time for preparations, but everyone was pitching in to make sure Connie had the best for her special day. An old aunt had already made the wedding gown, determined that no war was going to interfere with the tradition of a white bride. All the sisters were now busy making their own bridesmaid dresses, and George discovered that he had to take a back seat while all this activity was going on. Mr Lawrence looked ruefully at him.

'It's no good, George, when women get their minds set on a wedding, a mere man doesn't get a look in.'

Local Hero

On the wedding day itself, however, all their efforts were rewarded. Daisy Constance Virginia looked a vision as she walked down the aisle of St Andrew's old parish church in Enfield.

✎ 20 ✎

War on the Home Front

Zeppelins brought the war hideously to the home front in 1916. From the end of March these lumbering great airships were launched in attacks on London and surrounding districts, chugging across the sky like inflated cigars, showering bombs and incendiaries to flatten houses and create a war of nerves. On March 31st, seven approached up the Thames. Though it was a dark night, at least one of them was picked up in the beam of a search-light. Anti-aircraft guns immediately opened up, and the L.15 was crippled. It turned back, but soon lost height, eventually folding up and falling into the Thames estuary. The Lord Mayor of London paid out the £500 he had offered as a reward for the destruction of these raiders. But still they came, almost unmolested, either under cover of darkness or at altitudes beyond the range of guns on the ground.

Lady Orr Lewis had begun to entertain young officers at White Webbs as part of her contribution to the war effort. It was during a dinner party for men of the Royal Flying Corps that one young officer by the name of Leefe Robinson showed the way. The champagne flowed as the subject of dealing with Zeppelins became the topic of conversation. It caused some derisive laughter at first when Robinson declared that they could best be shot down from aeroplanes in flight. It had been tried before, of course, without much success – but not using incendiary bullets. His fellow officers ridiculed the idea, but Leefe Robinson was in earnest. He reminded them that fire was the airship's chief hazard, and that only the previous summer Flight Lieutenant Warneford had collected his VC for setting fire to a Zeppelin over Belgium by dropping an explosive bomb on to it, which set fire to the gas chambers.

Various pecuniary rewards, amounting to several thousand pounds, were offered to anyone who could find a way of combating the Zeppelins, but because of the great danger, both to pilot and plane, of attempting to shoot them down from the air, the exercise was not much encouraged by those in command. Robinson wagered that, on the next raid, he would succeed with his method of attack. Nobody took the wager very seriously, for even Leefe Robinson was not the sort who would lightly throw away his life for a bet. Even so, George had a feeling that this gallant young officer meant every word he had said.

A few days later, George remembered the young pilot's wager during a convivial Saturday evening at the Rose and Crown, and confided the incident to his friends. After closing time, several of them were invited to a late supper, for Mrs Lawrence had promised a baking of her renowned speciality – rabbit pie.

It was past midnight by the time dishes had been cleared away and the company had gathered round the piano for their favourite songs. Then, in the early hours of Sunday, September 3rd, 1916, the maroons were fired to indicate an impending air-raid. Though the night was dark, they went outside on hearing the sound of an airship's engines. Shortly afterwards the great balloon was picked up by searchlights. Artillery blazed into action, but it was plain to see that the shells were dropping short of their target. Then there came the sound of another engine and the big guns stopped firing. A lone plane flew into the arena, like a silver moth in the glare of the search-lights. Neighbours appeared outside to witness the David and Goliath battle. With guns blazing, the lone champion attacked his giant opponent and people cheered to see his astonishing display of aerobatics. There was one bright spark and the next moment the sky was filled with fire. The airship's gas containers ignited in the centre and flames roared to either end, a fearsome sight that silenced the cheering of the spectators. The outer covering began to peel back, leaving the glowing framework exposed, as the Zeppelin began to drift. Fired by revenge, a small crowd began to follow the stricken airship's slow descent, hoping to be at the spot when it came down. They followed over fields and through hedges, as the huge airship suddenly plummeted down, pieces falling from it all the time. Figures could be seen jumping out, making a desperate bid for life rather than dying in that inferno.

It came down in a field near Cuffley, reduced to a twisted, glowing skeleton. The crowd that now collected was held back by the fierce heat. The fire brigade arrived and played hoses on the charred structure. Then came the gruesome task of getting the crew out. The stench of burning flesh was sickening. George tried to tell himself that the man being dragged from the wreckage in front of him was a German, one who had come to kill and destroy, but as he was lifted the arms came away from the body, rather as one would pull the leg off a Christmas turkey. George felt suddenly ashamed, for himself and for his countrymen, some of whom were rummaging among the wreckage for souvenirs. One man pounced triumphantly on a cap badge, another on a half-burnt book. One even carried away the remains of a toilet seat in his eagerness to say at some later date 'I was there'. George had cheered as loudly as the rest, to see that young pilot strike a blow in defence of his country, but he wanted no souvenir of this terrible night. It was the second time that George had come face to face with war in its most cruel form and he discovered that he had no stomach for gloating over the enemy's misfortunes.

The following morning the newspapers were full of praise for the young Leefe Robinson. He was everyone's hero for his outstanding bravery and daring. A few days later it was announced that he had been awarded the VC. He also claimed some £3,500 in rewards, and the Lord Mayor of London put in a request to the War Office to be allowed to add another £500 to the award he had previously made for the destruction of the L.15.

So the SL.11 (not strictly a Zeppelin, but a rival Schütte-Lanz airship) went down in history as the first of these giant war machines to be shot down over Britain by a fighter aircraft. It was by no means the last. Another was brought down, not far away at Potters Bar, exactly one month later, and that was followed by a whole succession of Zeppelin kills.

Robinson himself was shot down over enemy lines in 1917 and taken prisoner. He died very shortly after his repatriation at the end of the war and a monument to his memory was erected on Cuffley Hill.

Although Arthur's letters from the fighting front were cheerful enough, George knew it was no picnic. Conditions were worsening every day and those returning with dreadful wounds, frost-bite and suffering from shell-shock all had tragic stories to tell. George would have given anything to be with his brother. He had always felt a responsibility towards him ever since they were children and now, when he needed him most, he couldn't be there. Babworth was a dismal place these days, with an unmistakable gap in the close-knit family. Their mother had framed the elaborately embroidered cards he sent; one in particular – a picture of a soldier dreaming of his mother – was embroidered with forget-me-nots and roses. The first letter George received breezily joked about France.

I can't understand it, our George, you going balmy about Froggy land. Where's all that sunshine you talked about? It's done nothing but rain since I've been here. The shell holes make lovely swimming pools though, and I'm thinking of taking swimming lessons.

In the meantime, the six months' deferment from work of national importance given to George was nearly up. The injury still gave him a lot of trouble. The bone, having knit badly, quite often slipped out of joint, giving hours of agony during the time he 'walked it' back into place. His own doctor declared him unfit to stand for any length of time, as one would have to do on a factory floor, but the Medical Board had failed him on a slight heart condition and this had now improved.

With the introduction of conscription, more and more men were shipped to the war zones every week. Enormous manpower gaps were left in industry and munitions and for the first time women were becoming a major force in the nation's production. Despite what his own doctor said, George felt certain that there would be no deferment this time. Sir Frederick, too, had done his best to keep him, and George knew this was not entirely selfish; he really believed that in his own vital work with the Admiralty, George was an invaluable asset. However, the battle was lost and George was directed to report to the Labour Exchange within the next two weeks.

George had never really considered his true worth to the Orr Lewis family until now. Lady Orr Lewis was distraught over his pending departure, and even Duncan, who never as a rule expressed sentiment of any kind, looked doleful.

'The old place won't seem the same without you, you old bugger.'

Sir Frederick assured George that his position would be waiting for him as soon as the war was over and, being rather sentimental himself, George was an unhappy man as he began to pack his trunk.

He was undecided whether to go back to Retford to be with his own family, or to seek employment in Enfield and stay in close contact with his young lady. It would have been ideal if he could have lodged with the Lawrence family, but the house in Gloucester Road was fully occupied and there simply wasn't room for him as well. Dorothy persuaded him to take lodgings with a neighbour, who had a small back room to spare, and to get a job at the same munitions factory where several members of the family were already employed.

George still felt that at least half his world had collapsed, as the footmen manoeuvred his large trunk down the staircase of White Webbs for the last time. He had debated whether to part with the trunk, now that he was leaving gentleman's service, but it had travelled many times across the Atlantic with him and, because they had been travelling light on that occasion, it was the only thing that hadn't gone down with the *Lusitania*. Out of pure sentiment, and because it now held his many souvenirs, he decided to keep it.

The whole household was gathered in the front hall to see him off. While Marshall loaded his trunk on to the Rolls, he went through the rather painful procedure of farewell. Everyone smiled and wished him well, being careful to keep that stiff upper lip. Only cook sniffed into her handkerchief, despite the fact that they hadn't always seen eye to eye over everything. Then he was on his way down that long drive to a new life – a life where he would be footing the bills instead of Sir Frederick, a life in which he would be his own master, but with all the responsibility that goes with it. All those who talk glibly about servants in bondage and having their freedom would have received some curt answers from George that day.

His new landlady, Mrs Pidgeon, greeted him cordially enough and led the way up a narrow flight of stairs to a small back room, where a single bed, a chest of drawers and his trunk, was about all the space would accommodate. It almost gave him claustrophobia, after the spacious surroundings he had been accustomed to, and the stale odour of fried fish from downstairs did nothing to raise his spirits. It was a pleasant enough little house and the woman seemed clean and homely, but as he began to unpack, he felt homesick, not for his parents' cottage in Babworth, but for his own quarters in White Webbs. At this moment, he felt like a wolf cub who had been reared by hand and then thrown back to the pack, full of apprehension and uncertain whether he would be accepted.

Over the weekend, the Lawrences took him under their wing. It was arranged that, apart from bed and breakfast, he would spend the rest of the time with them. This suited him much better – until Dorothy and he could get married and set up a home of their own. He soon settled into the family atmosphere and adjusted to this new sort of life. Mealtimes were fun, with all of them assembled round that very large table, enjoying the leg-pulling while Mrs Lawrence served the food from large tureens and Mr Lawrence presided from his place at the head of the table. It was almost like being back in the servants' hall.

He began work as a machine hand at the Enfield Small Arms factory. At first, the noise, the smell of grease and the general wear and tear on his nerves was almost unbearable, but with the high spirits of Pete Lawrence, who also worked there, he soon made new friends and a satisfactory wage, as he slowly became proficient at the work of making trigger guards. George began to feel he was useful after all.

'Didn't I say you'd manage it all right?' Pete reassured him. 'It doesn't need too much skill. If I can do it, any bloody fool can.'

George laughed; it was the nicest back-handed compliment he had ever had.

Dorothy began to prepare her trousseau for their wedding early in 1917. Letters from George's brother Arthur in Flanders indicated that some leave might be possible about April and he hoped to be best man. A short holiday spent at Babworth just before Christmas of 1916 filled George with nostalgia. He went to visit old friends in service to Rufford and Welbeck but found nearly all those of his own age away in the fighting line, some never to return. Much of the vast gardens had now been grassed over, due to the lack of staff, and the huge vinery, that had been his brother's pride, looked untidy and neglected. Even the little pub at Ollerton seemed to depress him with ghosts of the past and only made him miss his brother more. However, on his return to Enfield, a letter from Arthur relieved his low spirits to some extent. It was full of the prospect of his leave and of the wedding and he assured George that he would be there to see him 'spliced' if he had to swim back.

'You get the beer in, George, I'm a bit sick of muddy water, it gives you webbed feet.'

Despite the shortages, George was determined that his bride should have the best wedding he could afford. Dorothy had her wedding gown ready for the great day and they had even managed to find unfurnished accommodation. Peppers, the Enfield car and carriage hire service, were well known to George. When the private cars at White Webbs had been out of action, he had secured a contract for Peppers to provide transport. He decided to remind them that they owed him a favour. He told them he wanted the best turn-out they could provide. But in the middle of all the excitement came the telegram that blighted George's happiness.

We regret to inform you, that Arthur Slingsby has been listed as missing, believed killed in action.

He went at once to Babworth to give what comfort he could, but found his mother dry eyed and withdrawn. Anxiously, they awaited further news, hoping that Arthur would be found alive. A few days later, a letter from the War Office confirmed that he had been taken from the battle field and into a military hospital in France suffering from pneumonia, where he had since died from his condition. They returned his few possessions and a bronze plaque to commemorate his service. Then his mother did cry, long and hard, as though her heart would break. On Sunday morning, Sir Albert Whitaker gave tribute in Babworth church to another of the estate's sons, who had given their lives in the service of their country, and Arthur's name was added to the roll of honour. That night, in the small bedroom where he and his brother had shared childish secrets and giggled under the bed-clothes, George gave vent to his own feelings and it was a saddened man who travelled back to Enfield three days later.

It was debated whether to postpone the wedding, but to do so would undoubtedly entail the loss of their precious new home. A lot of money had been spent on furnishings and all the other things needed when one sets up house. All the arrangements had been made and George knew that Arthur would have deplored any fuss on his behalf. He was going to be missed just as much in six months' time as he was in just six weeks, so the plans were not changed. The wedding day was booked for April 13th, 1917. In the next few weeks George threw himself into his work, volunteering for all the overtime he could get. Pete Lawrence was a tower of strength and had agreed to be best man at the wedding, though he, too, was under draught to join the Middlesex Regiment. Jack Lawrence, the eldest son, had survived right through the war and, although he had been treated for mustard gas burns, was still considered fit enough to continue his service. Mr Lawrence had recently lost his only brother in the battle of 'Hill Sixty', so at least George was among people who could well appreciate his feelings.

Eventually the wedding day arrived and George's associates in the car hire business made it the wedding of the year in the Lawrences' neighbourhood. Dorothy looked the equal of any of the titled ladies George had seen, in her ivory slipper satin gown. She carried Madonna lilies and her yards of veiling were held in place by real orange blossoms, brought home in cold storage by a friend of George's who was still in gentleman's

service. On her father's arm she rode to St Andrew's old
parish church in a carriage lined with white silk and
drawn by a perfectly matched pair of greys. It was
enough to brighten an otherwise overcast day and only
George felt a pang of sadness. Not a single member of his
own family was there to see him take that important step
in his life, owing to his mother's poor health. But he gave
no indication of these feelings as he arrived at the church
to await his bride.

Inside the church, the Reverend Mayers stood with a
soldier and his sweetheart. The vicar quickly explained
that they had a special licence to marry before the soldier
rejoined his regiment on embarkation the next day and,
to give them as much time as possible together, he
wanted George's permission to share the same wedding
ceremony. Of course, George agreed, and when Dorothy
arrived with her bevvy of pretty bridesmaids, Mr
Lawrence volunteered to give both brides away. Taking
one on either arm, he escorted them down the aisle to
the strains of the wedding march, two such different
brides, one in flowing white satin and the other in her
'Sunday best', but both sharing the flowers, the music
and the blessings, as they were brought to the altar
under God's holy ordinance.

As they waited, George looked at the young soldier
and they smiled at one another, then as their respective
brides reached the altar rail, the sun came out, sending a
shaft of sunlight through the stained glass windows to
bathe them in a pool of rainbow colours. At that
moment George had the curious feeling that Arthur was
present after all, that young soldier, standing so straight
and proud, could easily have been his brother, and
George almost choked on his emotions. The service
proceeded, they took their vows together, they signed
the register together and together they walked out of the
church to the triumphal music of Mendelssohn, into the

sunshine. As the bells of St Andrew's peeled out, they cordially wished one another happiness and, as the two men shook hands, George pressed a sovereign into the soldier's hand and whispered 'Have a drink on me, mate.'

Epilogue

From that moment hence, George's life was no different, in the main, to that of a great many others who had struggled through 'the war to end all wars'. They settled in their new flat, and with Dorothy's flair for needlework and design, it soon became a happy, comfortable home. They both continued to work, hoping to save enough to purchase their own house, but Dorothy became pregnant and all else was shelved to prepare for their first-born. They were happy and content with life at this moment, but the old Irish lace-maker had not only been able to predict the *Lusitania* disaster, she had also given a true prophecy of his future.

'Ye won't always be as well off as y'are now,' she had said, and George's status did change considerably immediately the war ended. Like thousands of others, he was made redundant and, with the remnants of humanity limping back from the battle fields, work of any kind was impossible to get. Then three personal disasters nipped the middle out of George's life, following in quick succession. First, the baby they had both anticipated with joy was born prematurely and lived only a few hours. In this age, George's son would have been nurtured in intensive care to full health and strength; as it was he whimpered away his life in only the warmth of his mother's arms. Immediately after this, their home was bought over their heads and they were given notice to quit without the option of alternative accommodation. Then came the news of Sir Frederick Orr Lewis's death. Lady Orr Lewis sold the estate to the local authorities and the family went to live in the south of France, thus dashing George's hope of going back into their service. But gentleman's service, as George had known it, was virtually over anyway. Those who had suffered four years of war wanted what they had been promised, a world fit for heroes to live in, while those who had earned substantial wages on the home front were now not inclined to enter the more restricted life in service. Even the gentry were having to change their once strict routine, and were hanging on to their oldest retainers; George's chances of being able to resume his profession were remote, especially now he was married.

For many months they lived in rented rooms, with George plodding back and forth to the Labour Exchange, but eventually he found employment with a motor works. Then a bachelor friend of Pete Lawrence's, whose father had died, offered them a home and, with Dorothy keeping house and George in a steady job, life began to look a little rosier, for those in any sort of full employment were lucky, with redundancy rife everywhere. Men with rows of medals pinned to their ragged clothes now sold matches and shoe laces at the corner of the street, while others trudged, unshaven and down at heel, from one end of the country to the other, begging food and doing odd jobs, so they could send a little money back to their near-starving families.

For the next few years George's luck held fast and, in time, Dorothy became pregnant again, this time giving birth to a healthy daughter, whom they named Nina. In truth, they would have preferred to start a family in a house of their own, but since nature had decided otherwise, the baby became the pivot of their lives. Dorothy knitted and sewed for all she was worth to keep Nina looking like a princess and every Sunday morning, while Dorothy prepared the lunch, George would take his new daughter out for an airing. This caused some amusement for his pals, who seemed to think there was something odd about a man pushing a pram, but George thought a man whose dignity wouldn't allow him to push his own child didn't deserve to have one.

However, trouble caught up with them again when, for the second time in their lives, the house they lived in was sold to the highest bidder. Again they searched for a home, but people were not so inclined to let to couples with young children, and the list for corporation houses was a long one. Nothing could be promised for at least six months, and in the meantime they were obliged to live apart in separate accommodation. The only way they could meet and talk was by walking round a near-by park and, with the baby cutting teeth and Dorothy fretful, it was an unhappy time for George.

Six months of this was enough. As they were no nearer to the top of the housing list, they decided to sell their furniture which was in store and go back to George's part of the country to try their luck there. With the pram packed with baby clothes and a few personal possessions, Dorothy caught the train to Retford, leaving George to follow at some later date when he had settled everything.

Although nothing was said, they both inwardly squirmed at the thought of having to live off George's parents, if only for a time, but George's sense of responsibility was stronger than his pride and the tiny cottage in Babworth was now their only salvation. To say that the arrangement was a happy one would not strictly be true. George's parents were set in their ways and Dorothy was determined to stick to hers. It was soon apparent that they had merely exchanged one problem for another. Dorothy didn't altogether understand the rather narrow outlook of the country way of life and they, in turn, thought of her as a frivolous Londoner. She wouldn't wear the sensible clothes more suited to her rustic environment and she liked a dab of powder on her nose. Because of this, many on the estate thought she was flighty, and the more they criticised, the more Dorothy was determined to go her own way. For George, life was anything but peaceful. He took casual work waiting at tables for big business dinners at places such as Cutler's Hall in Sheffield; it wasn't much, but his training in service helped to keep him in demand.

Nina was toddling now and needed four pairs of eyes to see that she didn't come to grief. The deep open well in the yard was a constant source of anxiety to Dorothy, but her parents-in-law thought she fussed too much. They told her repeatedly that she coddled the child and offered advice on her up-bringing, which Dorothy bitterly resented. What with his wife complaining about his mother, and his mother doing likewise about his wife, it was an impossible situation for George. The climax came when the butcher was called in to kill the pig. Dorothy was horrified at the cold-blooded attitude to this deed. She was extremely fond of all animals and often fed the porker with tit-bits over the sty: to have the creature slaughtered, as it was done in those days, in their own back yard, seemed to her nothing short of barbaric. It was the last straw. She packed everything in the pram and went to stay with a woman she had come to know on the other side of Babworth estate, leaving a note for George to tell him she would only return when they had a place of their own.

As it happened, it was the best thing Dorothy could have done. Within the next few weeks they were granted a council house because they were living apart and, when the dust of conflict settled between Dorothy and her in-laws, they began to build a new home at 1 Leafield Road, Retford. George found employment as a machinist and, apart from one other bad patch, when George had an accident at work which amputated two of his fingers, life continued normally.

Their second daughter was born in 1937 and they named her Marion. Nina had dearly wanted a brother, but Marion was a lovely baby and her grandmother adored her on sight. George's father had died a few years previously, so the grandchildren had now become an important part of her life, which ultimately created better understanding and relations all round.

A year later Mrs Slingsby died of a stroke.

In February 1939 the benevolent Mr Lawrence also died, leaving Dorothy's mother facing difficulties in keeping the old home going. On just ten shillings a week widow's pension, it was hard to make ends meet, and Dorothy, who had never really settled to country life, took the chance to get back to her own people. She and George gave up their home to take charge of 41 Gloucester Road, Enfield, and George took the position of steward at the Enfield golf club.

By the end of that same year, England was again at war with Germany and George did his bit as street leader with the local fire-watchers. At the end of the

Epilogue

war, the club closed down and George, now in his late fifties, found himself once again out of work. A former member of the club then re-claimed his house which had been requisitioned throughout the war and offered George the job of gardener, which he accepted gratefully. In the years that followed, his employer made the pleasant discovery that there was more to this new gardener than merely 'green fingers'. When a catering firm let him down over an important dinner party, George was able to shed his wellingtons, change into a dinner jacket and serve dinner to perfection. He organised it so well that the catering firm was never needed again.

There were many people who knew and liked the quiet and friendly Mr Slingsby, who pedalled his bicycle back and forth to work each day, though very few knew of his previous life among the rich and royal. George was drawn briefly into the limelight again in 1965, on the fiftieth anniversary of the *Lusitania* disaster. Reporters from the London *Evening News* and the *Enfield Gazette* arrived on the doorstep, both requesting his account of that terrible day in 1915. They took photographs of him, of his old passport and of the watch that had been in his pocket on the day he had struggled for life in those icy waters. Both papers carried his story that same day and then the BBC interviewed him on their programme *Today*. In a clear voice, George recalled vividly the great liner going down. He would have been a valuable asset to the film documentary the BBC was preparing for television, and indeed he was asked to take part in it. But George had been forced into retirement by an illness that grew steadily worse and, before he could make his television début later that year, he suffered a cerebral stroke and was taken into hospital.

On June 9th, 1967, George Slingsby, gentleman's gentleman, at the age of 78, was called to serve in the greatest house of them all.